Much More Than Sexuality

Much More Than Sexuality

Listening to
70 Gay People
Talk About Their Lives

Compiled and Edited by
Liz and John Sherblom

Audenreed Press

The poetry of Gordon Barker is excerpted from his book,
Where the Wind Blows Free...Reopened, 1989,
and is reprinted by permission of his estate.

Library of Congress Catalog Card Number 96-83147
ISBN 1-879418-90-8

Printed on recycled paper in the United States of America
First printing 1996

Audenreed Press
P.O. Box 1305, #103
Brunswick, Maine 04011
(207) 833-5016

We dedicate this book to the memories of

David Sherblom

Al Seymour, Jr.

and

Gordon Barker

and to their families and friends.

May we each better understand.

CONTENTS

PART 6 --

ACKNOWLEDGEMENTS

Undertaking this book would have been a far more daunting task without the support and encouragement of key people in our lives. In this regard, we gratefully acknowledge the continuous support and enthusiasm of our families and friends throughout the duration of this project. In particular, we wish to thank John's mother, Ruth Sherblom, for her insightful reading and comments on both an early draft and the nearly final draft. We also thank Liz's children and their wives/partner: Bill and Alyssa Gause, John and Phoebe Gause, and Rick Gause and Kristen Anderson for their belief in the book from its inception and for their invaluable suggestions as it progressed. Thank you also to John's sister and her husband, Becky Sherblom and Mark Goldstein, and to John's brother and his wife, Donald Sherblom and Martha Carpentier for their reading and helpful comments on an early draft of the book. We also want to thank Liz's father, Daniel Cotton, for his careful reading and thoughtful feedback on the overall presentation of the stories.

Our friend, John Silvernail, made many valuable suggestions and comments on this undertaking from its inception to its final draft. Thank you. We also thank Kristin Langellier, Karen Foss, and Ray McKerrow for their interest and helpful discussions throughout the process. And to the many other colleagues, friends, and family members who encouraged us along the way, thank you very much.

We can never thank enough Julie Zimmerman and her assistant, Will Nesbit, of Audenreed Press for their tireless work on the final editing of this manuscript. Without their enthusiastic vision and commitment to this project, this manuscript might have remained too unwieldy for any but the most dedicated readers.

We dedicate this book to Al, Gordon, and David, each of whom was a catalyst in its development. Al's story is included. Gordon became too sick to tell us his story before he died, but some of his poetry is included between each part. David died in July of 1989, but his spirit runs throughout the book.

Additionally, we dedicate this book to all of our interview participants who so generously shared their stories. We would also like to acknowledge the lesbian and gay friends and acquaintances who have influenced our thinking but whose stories are not included in this book. Thank you for your friendship, wisdom, and understanding. We further dedicate this work to gay people everywhere who live lives of quiet dignity and courage amidst our society's lack of understanding and acceptance of homosexuality as a natural part of the human experience.

Liz and John Sherblom
Spring 1996

LIFE, LOVE, SPIRIT:
AN INTRODUCTION

It was Christmas, and we were standing in the living room at John's parents' home. We had had to celebrate without John's brother, David, being present; and now the call came confirming what each of us had privately feared but hadn't dared discuss. David had pneumocystis pneumonia and we, as a family, for the first time had to openly discuss not only his AIDS, but his homosexuality.

Prior discussions of sexuality had been so uncommon in our family as to be virtually non-existent; but over the next two and a half years, we raised questions and talked more openly and acceptingly about sexuality, homosexuality, and AIDS. Out of the emotions and thoughts surrounding David's illness and eventual death, the seed for this book was germinated.

This is a book about human lives and spirit, about love and joy, about sadness, grief, and fear, about children, family, partners, friends, sexuality, homosexuality, and occasionally about AIDS. The stories told here are first-person accounts of being a lesbian woman or gay man in the United States today.

The origin of this book stands against a background of social and political debate about, and discrimination against, gay people as being somehow "different" or "other." At times in our lives, many of us have felt the pain of feeling different, other, or in some way unacceptable. Seeing ourselves falling short of the ideal or the expected is painful. How much deeper that pain for someone whose "difference" is officially stigmatized.

We each know ourselves as multi-faceted, complex individuals--the products of the myriad of influences that have shaped us from birth to the present. We are each unique personalities interacting with our environments on a multitude of levels. Most of us would not describe ourselves as fully explained by any one of those characteristics, although a particular characteristic may form a more or less dominant focal point in our personal or social development. Each of us is more than "the sum of our parts."

From the time we are young children, we are subtly, and not so subtly, guided toward male-female pairings. Children and adults who cannot or do not conform to this expectation often find themselves estranged from the people closest to them and sometimes from themselves. They are forced to spend an inordinate amount of time and energy trying to figure out what's "wrong" with them and why they don't feel the way everyone else apparently feels. It is hard to assess the personal and social costs of the loss of this energy that could otherwise be directed to discovering and developing the many other aspects of self. Much of this lost energy could be avoided if we, as a society, developed a constructive social norm around which to build a gay identity.

Each of us is influenced by, and in turn influences, the society in which we live. Human beings are created in many different ways, and we need to celebrate our diversity, rather than use it as a tool for divisiveness. We need to open ourselves to the multitude of possibilities for living positive, creative lives, and we need to teach our children the basic values of love and tolerance on which to build their lives.

Much More Than Sexuality offers an introduction to 70 very different people, many of whose only common characteristic is that they happen to be gay. Our intention in putting this book together is to facilitate a small step in the direction of re-examining people as fellow human beings, rather than as part of a group defined and stereotyped on the basis of one or another innate characteristic. In that respect, we hope that it adds to our oneness.

I hand to you all that is within me.
It's all I have to offer.

Hold it close and gently...
For if it is broken
The pieces will not fit into place again.

-- Gordon Barker

PART 1

Emily
Tony
Bill
Sheila
Mark and Matt
Susan and Betsy
Peter
Rick and Tommy
Jim

Emily

Meg hated to leave me. She worried about whether I could survive. Frankly, I think I've survived better than she could have. I remember her saying, "I want to take care of you, but if you die first, then I have a gun." She'll be dead five years this April, and it's still hard.

She was very attractive when she was young. She was born in 1920, during the flapper era. She had her hair short but not masculine, and she had beautiful eyes. She looked a lot like Nelson Eddie. She was very, very affectionate. Well, I shouldn't say affectionate, but if she liked you, you knew it.

I met her through my sister. I was born in 1914, so I guess it was in 1935. After about a year or so, I realized there was something growing there. I thought, gee, she's rather nice, you know. I sensed someone I could care for, but I didn't want to be involved in anything like that. To me, it was taboo. Actually, at that time I was dating somebody else, but eventually, we did get involved. Of course, she was very open about her feelings. I hadn't been aware of those kinds of feelings inside myself before that, because I was into men, too, and I was concerned about society. Then, we became attached, more or less, but we didn't live together at that time. You see, you had to be awfully careful. It wasn't like it is now. You still have to be careful, but then, it was almost criminal.

Back in '36 or '37, I was working, and Meg was engaged in the family business. It was the Great Depression, and I worked for my uncle just for bus fare. I think I got five dollars a week for five and a half days. Then after a couple years, another lawyer needed a secretary, so my uncle encouraged me to try for it. I went, and I was hired for $12.50. That was wonderful. We could get chopped meat for a quarter, so it's all comparable. I was there for a number of years.

I don't remember when Meg moved in, but for a long time, she did everything but sleep with me. She ate with me; she was there all the time. She was very busy at the business, and it got to be too much for her to run back and forth between her house and mine, so she suggested she sell her place and I sell my house and we buy one house with a swimming pool and everything we wanted in it. I agreed, and we lived there until we moved up here in 1971.

We had a ball. Our house was always filled with people. I always say the best time of my life was when I was between thirty-five and forty-five. Every weekend, our swimming pool was open, and our friends would come.

This was back in the sixties. That's almost thirty years ago, and people didn't accept you as you were, strange as it seems, but my group did. They figured, look, this is what we are. They didn't care. Outsiders would tolerate us, but they weren't accepting, let's put it that way. You had to block it out; it's the only way you could exist. When we went into public places, though, it was so evident that Meg was different. She was definitely masculine.

We'd go every week to see her mother, and her mother was mean. I don't think she intended to be mean, but she didn't understand. For instance, she was in the house one night when our neighbors came in. We were talking, and she made a reference to Meg. She called her 'it'. Our neighbor was furious. He never

20

spoke to Meg's mother again. He said to his wife, "I want no part of that woman."

Meg and I were exclusive with each other from the time we met, and I still feel her presence sometimes. I was in the kitchen watching TV recently, and out of the corner of my eye, I saw something that looked like a figure. I thought, "Hey, who's there?" I turned around and looked, and it disappeared. I feel that she's right here, but, gee, I'd love to see her.

Tony

Back in college, I remember one guy saying, "If you want to change the world, change your own life." That has stuck with me. To a great extent, my life revolves around my career of building, designing, and selling products for ecological homes. I'm into a healthy lifestyle and living lighter on the earth, although I'm not advocating living in caves. I think that we can have a lighter impact than we do and still have all the creature comforts.

I grew up in the Bronx. It was a real tight-knit Italian community. I had lots of cousins who lived right in the neighborhood, and we all went to Catholic school together.

My grandparents were still alive, and there were always parties at their house with incredible food. My grandfather used to make wine and had a wine cellar. My father and his brothers and sisters had a band, and they played whatever was popular. They had a good time.

What really strikes me is that back then, my parents and uncles, who would have been in their thirties, had plenty of leisure time. They were able to play and have fun. None of the wives worked. They owned an auto repair garage and gas station. They used to play at weddings and make money, but it was more that they were having fun. They were able to cover their gas, and they'd get a free meal. It was really a fifties view of the world--fun and dancing and an unawareness of social problems or political climate. Those were good times.

Before everybody left for the suburbs, the family was very tight. We were the first to move out. Then several others followed to different areas. That made the family spread out and not see each other as much.

In the Bronx, I played with kids in the neighborhood. When we moved to the suburbs, it was hard for me in many ways. I didn't fit in with the kids my age. I came from a homogeneous Italian, Catholic neighborhood and moved into an area that was mixed, with some Catholics, but a lot of Jews and Protestants. Everybody was from a different ethnic background. I would get taunted by the Jewish kids for being Italian. It's funny how the oppressed can become the oppressors. It bothered me, but there was one wonderful teacher. She said, "God made us all different ethnicities for variety, and don't let them bother you. You'll be in a situation where you won't be a minority some time in the future."

We were in that town for six years. Then we moved to New Jersey. I fit in better. I had a lot of friends, and most of my friends were Catholic. It was a good time. There was never any mention of homosexuality, except for George the florist, who was overtly effeminate. Of course, that's your stereotype. The gay man is either a florist or a hairdresser, and we didn't even have any gay hairdressers that I ever saw.

In high school there were about a dozen of us, mixed men and women, who hung around together. I was realizing that I didn't have a strong attraction to girls, but I didn't deal with it beyond that. I didn't allow myself to admit there was any attraction to guys. In many ways, I was the girls' closest male friend in the group. I was the one they could talk to in a different way than they talked to any of the other guys. I dated some girls too, but there was no magic there.

24

In college, it became more and more painfully evident, though, that if I wasn't totally drunk, there was just no possibility for sex whatsoever, but it was years trickling into my consciousness. I hear stories of people who knew when they were twelve. With hindsight, I can think back to kindergarten and being attracted to somebody. I can picture his face and remember his name, but that's with hindsight.

It really wasn't until I was traveling with some friends in British Columbia that I got in touch with those feelings. There were three of us, all men. They were straight and I was straight, except realizing that I wasn't. Part of it was just stepping out of my life. Just being there, with the pure water and the healthy living, knocked down all the little defenses I had built up in my head. There was no more denying my homosexual feelings.

Later on, I moved to Maine with this same group of friends, and I met my partner, Bill, at the Unitarian Church. They had gay-theme video parties there. I had seen him there and he looked interesting, but I had met this other guy and we were seeing each other a little bit. He was friends with Bill. Bill thought I was going out with this guy and that we were serious, so he didn't return my phone calls. For weeks I was calling and leaving notes on his door, and he wouldn't get back to me. Finally, he said that he wouldn't go out with anybody who was going out with a friend, so I had to get the friend to call him on the phone and tell him that indeed we weren't going out. We've been together now six or seven years.

I came out to my parents late. I figured it out when I was 28. I told them when I was 31. They seemed to take it okay, but they didn't really like talking about it, and I didn't shove it in their face. Then they were up a few summers ago. It was raining, and we didn't know what to do, so I said, "Well, how would you like to meet Bill?" They just said, "No, we hate that lifestyle." I said, "Well, what is that lifestyle?" My mother equated me with a child abuser and a rapist. This is kind of painful coming from your own mother. It really made me see that she had no idea who I was as a person.

My father is a Fundamentalist, and they have their anti-gay lines down pat. His reasons were your standard Leviticus crap. Once he started talking like that, I knew exactly what was going to come next. My mother's smarter and more well-read, so it really was a shock to hear that kind of bigotry from her. I guess that's why my father's comments didn't bother me as much as my mother's did.

I said, "It seems like you need to learn more about this;" and my mother says--and I swear to God she said this--"What do you mean? I know all about it. I watch Sally Jessie Raphael and Oprah." If she wasn't serious, it would have been hysterically funny. The kick is those are both pretty gay-positive shows.

It's fashionable now to bash your parents, and I could do that for hours, but to cut them a little slack, they've had their problems, and some of that baggage has been passed on to the kids. Hopefully, our generation will deal with it.

Bill

I'm a French teacher. When I first started teaching, I said nothing about my partner or my sexuality. Let people get to know me. The second year, they'd mention their partner, I'd mention my partner--no name, no gender. Third year, I brought Tony on a trip to Quebec with the rest of the faculty. It was like, oooh, that's interesting, but I got no garbage for it. A couple people had difficulty with it but never said anything.

We were sitting at a dinner table in a restaurant in Quebec, and one of the guidance secretaries asked, after Tony had gone to the bathroom, "Is he your um-um your husband, your um-um boyfriend?" I think she threw 'lover' in there, too. "Yes, partner. That's the word we use--partner." One of the men got slightly uncomfortable. He couldn't really deal with the subject. It was okay, as long as you didn't talk about it. In fact, I find that's a lot of people's perception. "It's okay, just don't talk about it."

I had a discussion with the chorus teacher a couple days ago--Greek Orthodox, fairly strict religious, and conservative. We had a major discussion over lunch, which is twenty minutes long. You have to get real deep, real fast. "What do you want to talk about it for? You always want to talk about it." I said, "Look up on your walls. See all those boy-girl images up there? You have a picture of your husband and your child on your desk. You tell me that you aren't talking about it?" I said, "Now, if you had some boy-boy images or some girl-girl images up on the wall, we

27

wouldn't need to talk about it." She said, "Oh, I get your point." These little things are so striking to someone who's not part of the "straight" world.

Tony and I met when I was in grad school. I'd taken a year off, come back to school, finished my degree in modern languages, and started my master's degree. He was part of a community living together, and I saw him at some sort of gay film showing at the Unitarian Church. I said, "Oh, he looks interesting." I found out later that he saw me and thought, "Oh, he looks interesting."

We didn't get a chance to talk to each other, because he was meeting all kinds of new people, and I was chatting with my friends. He was with a friend of mine, so I assumed that they were dating. I got a phone call from him a couple days later: "Hi, how you doing? Want to go for lunch or dinner, go for a walk?" I said, "Well, yeah, OK, sometime." Click. Then I found notes on my door, more phone calls, letters--all of which went unanswered--because I do not, DO NOT, mess with my friends' friends. That's one of the surest ways to become a pariah in the community--to mess with your friends' friends. He caught me once on the phone, and I said, "Look, until Charles tells me that you guys are not an item, you're an item." He said, "We're not an item. Call Charles. He'll tell you we're not an item." I called Charles. Charles is New Age, white bread. He can't refer to anything in a straightforward manner. I said, "So, are you and Tony an item?" He said, "Well, according to Sai Baba, when the moon's in the seventh house, like ummmmm..." so I hung up. Tony called me. I said, "Hey, Charles didn't say you weren't an item, so tough."

I was a grad student, and Thursday was my day off, so I slept in. I had a dumpy little two-room apartment with a shared bath across the hall. Eleven o'clock in the morning, Tony showed up with Charles in tow and came into my kitchen. He said, "So, tell him we're not an item." Charles starts going, "Well, Sai Baba says that when you eat the rice grains...." Total fruit loop. Anyway, it was obvious from that point on that, OK, you're not an item. I get it.

This was a Thursday, so we made a date for Sunday. We went out to dinner, and we've been together ever since. There was just something that said, "This is it." It's been perfect. There was just that energy, that click.

On my side, we have family support. He came home with me for Thanksgiving that first year. That was after only three weeks. He came the next Thanksgiving, too. He'd sleep in the guest room, and we'd sit on opposite ends of the couch, but each time we went home, we'd get a little closer. Then one time we were sitting at the kitchen table, and Mom was at the sink doing dishes. She said, "Oh, I got Tony's room all ready," and I said, "Tony will be sleeping in my room tonight." She had been facing us, and as soon as I said that, she turned around and starting doing dishes. There are two windows in front of the sink, so I could see the reflection, and it was like, CONSTERNATION--WHAT DO I DO NOW? Three minutes of WASHING THAT PLATE. Made sure it was real clean. She turned around: "OK." I chose my words carefully. I said, "In my room, not in my bed." You have to give them a chance.

After a few more times of sleeping in the same room, it was like, well, I'll put my legs over his legs while we're on the couch, and nobody cared; nobody said a thing. We don't discuss it, because why bother? If I brought a woman home, if I were straight, I wouldn't say, "Well, we're going to fuck tonight. It wouldn't be a topic, so why should it be a topic for me? I'm treating it as if I were living in an ideal world. I don't need to explain things that are normal for straight people.

My parents and I talk about Tony's and my relationship in the same way that we talk about my sister's relationship with her husband. It's funny to hear my mother's responses--to hear her say, "Well, you have to work on this and that. You have to be willing to try, and you have to be willing to give." She's treating us exactly as she would my sister and her husband. I'm hyper-sensitive about that type of thing, and it's been perfect.

His family is a disaster in terms of us. In fact, right now, they're on a non-communicating basis--his choice. The summer before last, they came up, and he said, "So, what do you want to do? Do you want to meet Bill?" Major family blow-out, and the deal is they can see him again when they choose to see me. Which is exactly the same proposition I would have made to my family.

****

I think growing up with the gay thing gives someone an inner strength, if they can survive it. Two-thirds of our teenagers are wiping themselves out, because they're gay, or they think they're gay. There are no decent role models.

There is the perception that gay people frequently out-perform their straight counterparts. The reasons may be: one, the repression that they experience causes them to have to work harder; and the other one may be just lack of constraints. Straight people, because they haven't had to question their existence on many planes and they don't have to question their sexuality, accept the roles society imposes and all those constraints. Whereas if I've questioned something, I'm going to question a few more things and say, "Oh, that doesn't apply to me, so I'm free." It gives you incredible movement.

On the other hand, one of our gay legislators, when she was running openly for her seat in the House, had had a really great day out on the old campaign trail. She is one of the most together people in the state, who rabid homophobes love, because she's so adorable. She was driving home in her little truck, and she said to herself, "Isn't everything wonderful. Things are going great. I've got the partner, the house; I've written books; I've got plenty of work; my politics are going great. If only I weren't a lesbian," and then she said to herself, "Where did that come from?" Internalized homophobia, just coming right out--BAM! That's in all of us. If it's in her, it's certainly in the rest of us.

Sheila

I was brought up Catholic. When I was twelve, I rebelled and wanted my own religion, so I went to the Pentecostal Church. I liked the music, but I didn't really believe. I've never really cared for churches or denominations, per se. I tried quite a few different religions, but there was always some way that I felt that each one discriminated. Discrimination's always been a big deal to me, because of who I am.

From the time I was eight until I was about twelve and a half, I lived in Virginia, and everything was separate as far as the "colored people" and "white people." One of my best friends in school was a black girl. It wasn't an okay thing to be friends with her, but somehow we worked around it. I felt really bonded with her, maybe because I felt like there was something wrong with me, and she felt excluded because she was black and wasn't supposed to associate with white people. I don't know what it was about for her, but I just always felt for the underdog, like we had something in common.

One thing I remember was when I was about thirteen, I was listening down through the registers. We had this big old house with these huge registers in the floor on the upstairs. I was listening to my mother and father talking, and they actually said that there was something wrong with me, but they didn't know what it was. That did me in, because then I really felt like there *was* something wrong with me, but they weren't telling me.

I was 21 when I realized I was gay. It was the best year of my life, as far as, "Now I know what's wrong with me!" When you don't know something, you have fears; you have uncertainty, hopelessness, despair, but at least when you know, you can deal with it. Not that I dealt with it very well.

I'd had plenty of signs to tell me I was gay. When I look back on it now, I can remember having feelings for kids of the same sex when I was eight years old, but it wasn't until I had an actual relationship with somebody that I knew what it was.

That relationship was very temporary, but it was very real, and it was really hard to experience the loss. It was the first person I was ever with. At the same time, though, I felt like I was human. I had had needs that had gone unmet for so long. At the ending of that relationship, which only lasted a couple months, I went right back to religion. I didn't deal with it well at all. I was really bouncing off the walls. It was like, "Oh, this must be bad. This must be wrong."

It took me a long time to come to the point where I accepted it for myself. I think I probably was in my 30s before I accepted it on all levels, especially on the spiritual level. I think the spiritual level was the toughest for me. I knew I was gay then, but I still had a reservation about whether God accepted me as I was. I don't feel that way now. I think that happened by just coming to terms with the realization that it wasn't a choice. It's like spending all those years fighting "this is who I am." I had probably also built a closer relationship with God, so that I felt like I was loved for whoever I was. I can't be somebody that I'm not. I don't think that would be kosher. I would be going against who I am, and I don't think that's what it's all about.

34

The thing that I have struggled with and still do today is just trying to be normal, trying to be real, trying to be human. There are things you can't do if you're gay or lesbian. You can't go in a restaurant, sit down with your lover, look into her eyes, and look like you're in love. It would be much easier for me to find somebody and us be able to stay together, if the world accepted us. You have enough to deal with on a day-to-day basis in your own life, never mind having to deal with this extra stuff.

I think it's changing, but we need to let people know that we are just human beings. We're not perverts. We're no different than anybody else. The only thing that is different is our sexual orientation. I think that's why I felt so close to that black girl when I was a kid, because I really can understand what she had to deal with.

As gay and lesbian people dealing with oppression, I think you deal with your life on a different level than people who maybe just go with the flow. Probably with any minority group, you have to really look at the emotional and spiritual sides of your life.

I don't like dealing with some of the struggles that I have had to deal with, but I'm grateful for who I am and that I'm gay, because it makes me sensitive to other people who get discriminated against. It gives me a whole different understanding. It's helped me to see that it has everything to do with the people doing the discriminating and nothing to do with me. There's been a lot of wisdom that's come out of it. I've learned to be true to myself, even though I stick out like a sore thumb. I've grown. I'm happy where I am, and it gets better all the time.

Mark and Matt

Matt: We do homophobia workshops. Homophobia is just so pervasive in this culture, but I think people are starting to get a clue, because you're seeing a change in the media and in the way things are portrayed.

Mark: We're fraternal twins, so the two of us go to groups and talk from a family perspective: nature versus nurture.

Matt: I've always been very close to Mark, but I knew early on that being gay was not a good thing. There were two definitions in the dictionary: gay means happy-go-lucky, gaiety; and then there was gay, being this really bad thing generally associated with men. I remember when I was seven or eight, looking at this huge book we had--a chronology of the sixties and seventies. There was a picture of two men hugging each other, and underneath there was this caption about the gay movement. My mom shut the book and said, "That's not a good thing."

I look at homosexuality as a genetic factor, and I think Mark and I are living proof of that. We were brought up in the same family; we were raised the same way; we received the same love from two loving parents in a very close family unit. We were exposed to very similar things.

Mark: But my coming-out process was very traumatic. It was this whole big thing that I had been carrying on my shoulders that I had never dealt with. I knew I was different from third or fourth grade. I knew there was something the matter with me, and I knew that I had to start watching what I did and how I acted. I had to not act like a sissy. I made conscious decisions in speech, manners, gestures, who I hung around with, and what I did. Everything had an implication to it. Throughout my life, I was always having to think about how others were going to perceive things, but at the same time, I came across as being a happy-go-lucky person. I channeled all of my energies into my artistic abilities.

In college, I took a human sexuality course. I had admitted to myself the year before that I was gay, and that was fine. Now I had to deal with how I was going to live my life, because that changed all of my plans and expectations. I had planned to become a priest, but that was ruled out now. I didn't want to put myself in a situation where I couldn't act on it, because even if my experience up to that point had been limited, I knew I was a sexual being. I had also begun to deal with the fact that I don't agree with everything the Church has to say on that.

At the same time, I was also finding that there were magazines with pictures and stories, and I was developing this little collection. It wasn't so much the sex that I was interested in as it was the fact that these people were admitting it and were supporting each other.

One time when I was away at college, my parents found some of these magazines that I had at home. I knew at some point they would. My mother doesn't pry, but my grandmother was coming to stay, and I had the nicest room. When they had tidied up, they found the magazines and looked inside.

It was shortly thereafter that the confrontation took place. I was home for Christmas. They called me in, and I knew immediately. I hadn't noticed anything different going on with my relationship with them, but when they called me in, they didn't say,

"We want to talk with you"; they wanted to talk *to* me. I knew that this was *the* thing that I had been dreading my entire life and for just reason. It was horrible. In our workshops, I spend a lot of time discussing it, because there are a lot of very powerful feelings that are still there, although I don't harbor anger any more. To sum it up, if you looked at all the negative things in my life--all the traumatic experiences--and pulled them all into one, they would not equal this one event. Even to the present day, adding in everything that's happened since then, it still doesn't equal that one event--not even close.

I don't remember how it started, and I don't know that my parents remember, because we just talked about this a month ago. I do remember that they said, "We found a magazine. What does this mean?" My mother has this real problem with pornography anyway, or "adult," as I would call it, so I knew that was working against me. Then they confronted me with the gay thing. It was obvious, because it was all explicit gay stuff, and it wasn't just one magazine. It was a three-pack.

They had gotten all the clues that I couldn't hide throughout my life and had denied it just like I had. This confrontation forced them to deal with it. I was extremely defensive. I said, "Well, I think I might be bisexual," because that was the lesser of the evils, even though I knew I was gay. I didn't volunteer anything. I had learned a lot through reading, but I instantly forgot everything that would justify me as a person. They went through the myths and said, "Well, I wouldn't want a gay teacher teaching my children. Gay teachers molest children, you know. Gay men molest children." I'm like, "No, that's not the case," but how could I back it up? They went through every male person in my life and said, "Is this somebody you did something with or had an attraction to?" I'm like, "How dare you? You have no right. This is my life. I may be your child, but you're overstepping some boundaries," but I couldn't say any of that. I was defenseless. I was so angry and caught unawares, so unprepared. Of course, were they prepared? I don't know.

They said, "At least we're not throwing you out on the street." My gut reaction later on was, well, maybe that would have been better. Here I had this incredibly close family that I had found tremendous support from, and now that was gone. Twenty-three years of my life were stripped away. No support. No nothing! They said, "What about God? The Bible says it's wrong." I'm like, "No, I can't believe that. I believe in a just God, a loving God. How can a God create me as somebody that's wrong, that's a horrible creature? I look at my identity, my sexuality, as a part of who I am." My mother was like, "Where did I fail?" I'm like, "It's nothing you did. You didn't fail. It's a genetic thing." If I'd been thinking, I would have said, "Matt's not gay. What's the issue? That's a proof right there," but I couldn't come back with anything. It seemed to me that it lasted for hours. I left; I felt like the whole thing was one-sided: them throwing stuff at me. It was a horrible experience.

Nobody talked about it after that. One thing I did say in that confrontation: "I have a couple books you could read that could open your eyes to things." They said, "No, we'll find our own resources." Of course, the first book that my mother turned to was written by a religious person and was totally against homosexuality: "It can be cured." After that, I said, "I have a lot of books, if you want to read." She said, "I've read enough. I'm tired of reading. I don't want to learn anything else, and I'm certainly not going to read anything you have to give me," although I don't think she remembers it quite that way.

Another thing they said was, "We want you in counseling." I said "No, I see no reason to go to counseling; I feel comfortable with who I am. Yeah, I have some things to work with, but I've made it this far. If I have a problem getting through my daily life, then maybe I'll go to a counselor for help doing that, but I don't see my homosexuality, or my bisexuality, as a problem. I certainly wouldn't go to somebody to get cured, because I don't see the need for a cure." They really pushed it. I thought, "Why don't you go to counseling, because I think you need it to help you deal with this," but I didn't say that. I didn't say much. I couldn't say much.

Matt was the first person that I ever told willingly, but it took me three hours in a car to tell him, even though we were in the human sexuality class together and we had worked as founding members on a committee to develop an organization that would be in tune to the diversified needs of sexuality on campus. There was still a lot for me to deal with. I knew I was gay, and I could accept that, but to share it with other people was a very difficult thing.

I understood right from the start that my parents would have a difficult time because of their upbringing, their knowledge, and their experience. They said that they still loved me, but I had a hard time believing it, because they weren't showing it. This is where Matt comes in, because that summer he worked at the same place my mother did. They would commute together and talk about things. They talked a lot about sexuality, because that's what Matt's field is.

Matt: I was in school, and I had gotten involved with the field of sexuality, which I knew pushed some of my mom's buttons.

41

I didn't do it to piss her off, but it was something that fascinated me. I've always been interested in socially conscious issues anyway. The human sexuality course gave me a chance to look at homosexuality.

I was a resident assistant on campus, and I had gotten to the point where I wanted to start doing programs around homophobia education. I made conscious efforts to really look at what I did and didn't do. Did I tell fag jokes? Yes, I did, occasionally. So then I did everything I could to become more sensitive to it. I was trying to develop myself as a better human being. The homophobia was part of it, and I got onto this committee with Mark, and we were looking at these issues. At that point, I still had no idea, although there was something in the back of my mind that said Mark was different, but I never looked at why or what.

When he came out to me, my first reaction was, "That's great; I'm happy for you," but inside, it bothered me. Now I can say that the reason it bothered me is because my expectations for Mark were lost. I guess I still had some of that stuff in there that said, "Maybe he won't be a priest and he'll have a family, and I can bring my kids over to his kids and vice versa."

We all have these expectations for people, whether we realize it or not. I realized it was the loss of my expectations, developed from living in a heterosexist society. I couldn't put words to it back then, but now I can. That bothered me for a long time. I kept wondering, "Why do I feel this way? I love him as a brother, and it's irrelevant what his sexual orientation is." One thing that struggle did was to give me more power, motivation, determination, and strength to continue doing my homophobia work. It really sensitized me to the whole issue.

42

Then I found out what a traumatic experience it was for Mark, and I went back to my mom. I started pushing her buttons every time I had the opportunity. She and I were both working weird hours at the same place, and she'd drive with me. It was about a 45-minute commute each way, so it gave us plenty of time to look at these things. I said, "I understand the pain you're going through," and we'd talk and talk and talk. I kept saying, "I have some books if you're interested," and I'd put out all the facts that I had at my disposal. I dispelled some of the myths, and we would talk about that. Over time, things got better. I really didn't talk to my dad, because my dad doesn't talk, but it got back to him through my mom. I think it was good for me; it was good for my parents; and it was good for Mark.

Mark: I feel strongly that the reason my relationship with our parents is back to what I want it to be is that we're open and communicating. They can ask me anything now, and I can be honest with them.

I would do homophobia workshops full time, if I could. I think a human sexuality course should be required, especially in college. If nothing else, it will open people up to some facts. It's not just about sex. It's about being a person. If somebody is gay, they should be able to act on it, accept it, and get on with their life. I see it as a real wall in somebody's life. I don't agree with "outing" a person as a practice, because I think people have their own time and place to do that, but my wish is for everybody to come out.

Susan and Betsy

Betsy: We're very blessed. We have a really good relationship, and we're very happy. We've had some tough times, just like any couple does, but we've ridden them out. We were very fortunate to find each other. It doesn't often happen, whether you're heterosexual or lesbian or gay, that you find someone you're so comfortable with, that you know that no matter whether you argue or not, there's never a question. It is absolutely unthinkable to me that I wouldn't be with her. It's just a comfortable reality.

Susan: I met Betsy in the federal program that she brought to her city. She was looking for people to work with this innovative grant that she'd gotten for a high school library.

Betsy: That was back in the sixties, when we had money for education.

Susan: So I went to work for her for three years. Then I got fired, because it became obvious to everyone...

Betsy: ...that we'd fallen in love.

Susan: We fell in love, because we shared so many of the same values and beliefs. The excitement of the work spilled over into our personal lives. It was a staff of ten, and everybody loved everybody else in some ways, but ours went a little beyond what everyone else felt.

Betsy: I was a married woman with three kids, and I was not expecting to fall in love. It was the farthest thing from my mind. It just happened.

The principal of the school liked us both, but he decided that we shouldn't be on the job together. He had heterosexual couples working in the school system, but because he figured that we were gay, he couldn't possibly allow us to continue to work together. It bothered him a lot to have to tell us, and he cried about it.

Then, I had to make a big decision all by myself. I hadn't even talked to her about it, but I knew that something had happened and that I had to deal with it. I spent a long weekend just thinking about it and finally came out, remembering something really wonderful my mother had said to me. I don't even remember the question that occasioned the answer; I only remember her saying to me that some women preferred the company of other women, and some men preferred the company of men. It seemed so calm and objective and matter-of-fact that it was there in the back of my head, and it came up when I started trying to find out what it was that was happening to me. Is this a terrible thing or what? I thought, "No, love is not a terrible thing. Love between two women is just a matter of their preference. What's the big deal?" So, I went forward with that in mind, and it helped me a lot.

It didn't help me all the time, because there were mornings when I would wake up, and I'd think about my son, in particular, and say, "What have I done? Why am I not leading this life that I was leading before, which was the great American dream?" It was the husband and wife, three kids, the swimming pool, two cars, a big house and cocktail parties.

I had grown away from my husband, though, and I probably would have left him sooner or later anyway. I used to think to myself, sometimes, when I was going to sleep at night, "Is

46

this it, then? You get married, you have kids, then you see these same people at these same parties, and you say the same things to each other, and Saturday night you have sex, and Sunday morning you get up and have waffles." That was the way it was. Then, when Susan came along, it changed and became such an incredibly different picture for me. Everything opened up. I was given another life. It's like I died and had another chance.

My son chose to stay with his father, although when I left, I told him I was going to build a house on the other side of the patch of woods, within very quick walking distance and that he was welcome to come and stay there, or he could come and visit whenever he wanted.

Susan: She took the youngest child with us, so we raised her together. Then the middle daughter went away to school.

Betsy: That was the roughest time for us, when we first made that transition into living together in a community where we were an open scandal, where she had been let go from the school, and everybody knew the reason why. We lived in a residential, but somewhat rural, neighborhood, and my daughter would get invited to a Christmas party with her father, who lived next door, but we would be left out. Our neighbors didn't speak to us. I would go to children's events at my daughter's school, and the parents of the neighborhood would be sitting in the same row with me or in front or in back of me, but they wouldn't speak to me. I was really an outcast for a while.

On the job, people were very accepting. I did my job and got along well with everybody. I was never discriminated against at work, but in the neighborhood, I had liberal friends whom I really loved. I thought they were going to be the bulwark for me, but I was so mistaken. I still wanted social acceptance, because I was still me--the same person that I'd always been. I had moved in "the privileged" circles of society and then suddenly became an outcast. It's a damn good lesson for you. I mean, everybody should go through it, because they'd be humbled a little bit.

People are always saying to me something about how I just found out that I was a lesbian when I fell in love with Susan. I don't look at it that way at all. I feel like I made the choice to love her, that I fell in love with her in the same way I might have fallen in love with some man. On the other hand, for Susan, I know it's different.

Susan: I've been gay since I was ten, but this relationship was something that happened very gradually, as we developed this mutual admiration society and friendship, this real partnership and community of purpose.

For me, though, I remember standing in my bedroom, when I was ten years old, and saying to myself that I will not allow anything or anybody to tell me that I can't be what I want to be in this life. I already felt as if things were getting kind of scary. My mother was very, very angry, and she was verbally abusive and physically abusive on occasion. She knew that I was a lesbian. She was an alcoholic, but she was very smart, and she had figured out that some of the relationships that I had in high school were far more than just friendships.

There were people who saved my life all along the way, though, and one of them is my aunt, who's 83 now and who has been one of those Rogerian unconditional love people. I think the only thing that would have made her turn against me--although she still would have been there for me--is if I'd become a mass murderer or something. Literally, every person in my family has

48

been saved by her from the ravages of our parents, who were both alcoholic. Auntie was a social worker, and she took us everywhere with her. I think you'll find that most gay people have somebody who was there, who helped them survive and feel good about themselves, whether they knew about their sexuality or not.

It's taking risks to be a lesbian, but to identify with an oppressed group is something that I'm willing to do, because I am a member of that group. On the other hand, I never identify myself as a lesbian to myself. I mean, I'm a teacher, a department chair, a sister, a daughter, a granddaughter, a niece; and I'm all kinds of things in relation to Betsy, as well as her friend and lover. I've thought a great deal about it, and I've read a great deal about it. I don't consider it to be homophobic to identify with the many other different roles that I play in life. I'm all kinds of things.

Peter

I worked as a therapist at a counseling center for three years. I'm not sure whether those people's lives changed, but mine did. Those were the years of giving up the pretense, getting a divorce, and my then ex-wife taking her life. I had reached a point where I realized that this pretend person wasn't me. Not that everything was a pretense. I love my kids, and I can't imagine life without them, but I wasn't a straight man, and I was terribly unhappy.

I'd gotten married to be normal. I thought I could pull it off. I thought I could do this and have the family that I wanted and bury the other sexual questions and issues. It might be difficult at times, but it was worth the price. Not true! I didn't have sex with anybody outside of my marriage, but I realized that this was not who I was, that I was terribly unhappy, that in the process I was damaging everybody else as well, and that it was time to bow out.

Before we got married, I had been straightforward with my wife about my sexual history and that I had some real concerns. In that sense, everybody went into it with their eyes open, but on the other hand, I don't think you can really know. You think you can do it; she thinks she can "convert" you or keep you satisfied. You both try, but it just doesn't work. So, when five and a half years later, I said this was it, there was some foundation; but I don't think it made it any less painful.

It was a very difficult decision for me for a number of reasons. One was the choice of daring to live this "unacceptable" lifestyle. The other very significant reason for me was, if I do this, do I lose my children in the process?

There were some other pieces to that. My ex-wife, aside from being a woman, had a significant mental health problem: she was bi-polar. That got tangled up in the whole thing, because I couldn't say to myself, I bow out of this, and, knowing how the courts stand, the kids are all going to go with her. I couldn't do that and feel that they would be adequately or properly cared for. There was a real risk that they could be harmed. She refused to take any medication and when she was depressed, she became homicidal as well as suicidal. That compounded the difficulty of making the decision. I finally decided to go all the way--not only did I want a divorce, I wanted the kids. I got two of them. The two older boys went with her, the two younger ones with me.

The house belonged to me through money I'd inherited, so I stayed in it. She moved out in October; we were divorced in March; and two and a half years later, she committed suicide. At that point, the two older boys came home. So we went through this odd shifting back and forth--we were one family with four kids; we were two families with two kids each; and then, all of a sudden, we were one family with one parent and four kids.

After my ex-wife died, I ended up taking almost a five-year block of time off. I stayed home, raised the kids, and ran the farm. After everything they had been through, I was concerned that the boys have a parent around on a full-time basis. Even though things were tight, if I was careful, we could make it. After they were all in school and pretty well settled, I went back to work.

It was important to me to be a good father. I consciously worked at not doing some of the things that I saw my father do. I look back on it and can say I actually did a good job of not duplicating what he did, but in the process of not duplicating that, I messed up a few other things.

I think no matter how many skills you have, there are innate differences between men and women. I'm a good cook and a mediocre housekeeper. I can sew; I can knit; I can wash the dishes; I can make beds. I can do all of those things, but I'm simply not a mother. I look at my grown sons and see what not having a mother has done. They're all very independent, very self-sufficient. I suspect that at a certain level, they may be difficult to get close to. I watch them in their relationships. They date, and two of them have girls they've gone out with for a long time; but I think it's difficult for them to know how to have a relationship with a woman, because they don't have that experience. They were very young when their mother died.

It's difficult, because you end up looking for somebody to blame. I am the way I am, because my mother overcooked the spaghetti. It has to be somebody's fault. My own feeling is that yes, what our parents do to us or the way they are may not be as we would like it to be, and we may get to adulthood with some scars and some holes, some gaps or some raw spots, but eventually, we all have to reach the point of saying, "OK, these things happened. Now we are adults and we are responsible for what we do." We have to stop blaming.

As a parent, I have to do the same thing and say, "I may not have been a perfect parent, and I certainly apologize to you for the things that were not as they could or should have been; but you're a big boy now. The only thing we can do is make peace with whatever that past was and make the best of the present." That's the way I feel when I look back on my life and certainly on trying to be a single parent. I did some things well. I didn't do some things terribly well. I can't go back and change any of that. I can only go on.

I look back on the past, and there are periods of time, moments--and this may seem like an odd word to use--that were incredibly sweet. There are times I wish I could recapture for just a little while. I love little kids and miss having them around. There's a joy to bringing home some very simple present and having that be wonderful. Once in a while I'd like to step back and recapture that, yet there's something exciting about finding out what's going to happen tomorrow. I'm at the point where I'm ready to be a grandfather.

****

For me, growing up an only child was significant. I don't know whether other only children feel the same way, but I felt a terrible sense of aloneness. I can remember when I was six or seven begging my mother for a little brother or sister. I didn't care which; I just wanted a companion. On top of that, though, I was also dealing with feeling different from everybody else. I'm not sure when, but I knew in high school. One of the memories that I have is lying in my bed, thinking, "I do not want to be this way." So I know I knew then, but I can't tell you when I figured it out.

A lot of the not wanting to be gay probably had to do with the fact that being gay negated a lot of other things I wanted in life. I always wanted to have kids, to have a family of my own. It seemed to me, then, that if you were gay, then you could not have a significant other, be part of a couple, be loved, and be cared for, despite wanting that very much.

54

And I didn't want to be something that's this unacceptable. It infuriates me when I hear people say that it's a choice. The only choice involved is when you finally choose to be who you really are. You certainly don't choose what that is. That's a very difficult choice, when who you are isn't acceptable, when who you are potentially costs you the things you want most in life.

I've since learned, though, that I was wrong about a lot of what it would mean to be gay. I haven't given up any of the important things. When I made the decision to live my life honestly, I went all the way. I don't flaunt my sexuality, and I don't hide it; I just live. If there's an office party and spouses are invited, I bring mine and act as though nothing's out of the ordinary. Eventually people begin to see that your house has more than a bedroom.

I've been a child protective worker for a number of years. I've been a 4-H leader, sat on teacher selection committees, sat on the town redevelopment committee, served on several state committees. I founded an HIV/AIDS social service agency that serves over a third of the geographic area of the state. I have more friends than I ever did when I was pretending to be someone else. And I have someone I love, who loves me. I have a partner in every sense of the word that I ever dreamed of. Scott is a lot younger than I am, and he's struggling with the same stuff I did so many years ago, as well as with AIDS and knowing that he doesn't have much time left. I want to make the most of the time we have, however long or short, and I hope when we reach the end that we both know is coming, he's found the contentment with himself and the pride that he deserves. For the rest of my life, though, I'll know that I was loved and that I loved in return.

I honestly don't understand what's behind non-acceptance. It doesn't make sense to me. It makes sense when the other person is doing something that's harmful to you, but being gay causes no harm to anyone.

Rick and Tommy

Tommy: I'm not one to brag, but I think we have one of the healthiest relationships I've ever seen. We don't fight about anything. We don't bicker. We're not jealous. We're just a married couple.

Rick: After work, we come home, we cook supper, and we decide either to go shopping or watch TV, or we have someone over or go over to someone's house.

Tommy: We feel similar about the same things in life, even though we're not the same age. I'm just turning 24, and Rick's 39.

Rick: That could be a hard situation, but we let each other be their own person, and we enjoy working together on our projects. We like going to yard sales, antique shows, and flea markets. We've got one of the rooms in the attic stuffed full of collectibles for when we have a bigger house.

Tommy: For the future, I guess we've just got basic, boring needs. We want to get rich, have a house, live in Florida in the winter, and come to Maine in the summer.

Rick: We've got a couple apartment houses, so they're going to help us a lot, financially. We want to make all we can in the next seven years. This place will be paid for, and when it's paid off, we'll have enough to retire on. We won't retire completely; we'll always be working for ourselves, but I call that retirement. We're working for that future together.

Tommy: Recently, when Rick's parents came home after being away, we went out to visit them, and Rick's father came

right over to me and gave me a big hug. I'm like, "Oh, my God."
It just totally blew me off my feet. I didn't expect anything. His
father is really, really nice.

Rick: I noticed at the time that Mom was about to, too,
but she's uncomfortable.

Tommy: Yeah. I don't think his mother really likes me
too much.

Rick: She does, but she was uncomfortable. This is
something new to all of us, anyway--hugging, saying "I love you,"
and all of that. I can't remember what brought it about, but
different people say, "My father died, and I never did get a chance
to say I loved him," or whatever. Anyway, that hit home a few
times, and we all decided that that was a pretty good thing and that
we should be doing this, and how come we weren't? So we do,
more so. Now Mom will say things like, "I think Tommy's good
for you," and, "it's nice to see you with someone that's helping you
do things that you need to do." In the past, I never had that, and
she appreciates it. It makes a difference that my family likes
Tommy. It makes the relationship easier.

Tommy: I don't have the same rapport with my family
that Rick does with his. My family doesn't call all the time. I
don't even talk to my family once a month.

****

Tommy: As a kid, I was "out" in school. I came out in
eighth or ninth grade, because I was provoked. I always knew that
I was attracted to boys, and everybody always thought that I
looked like a girl. It wasn't until tenth grade that I started getting
friends.

I really thought that I was in love with a woman in high school. We were best friends. We never had sex, but we were always fooling around. She paid attention to me, and we always did things together. Still, I knew that I was attracted to men. At the beginning of our senior year, we said, no more. I just told her, "I like men, and you're not a man."

Rick: Everyone expects you to have girlfriends, so you try to have girlfriends. I remember when I worked at a cafeteria, some of the women were talking about this man being "queer," and one of the women said, "Well, there are men that like other men." All of a sudden, it dawned on me, "Oh, yeah, there are, aren't there. That's me." It's like you always knew, but all of a sudden, you just woke up. It's like a bad joke, and after a while, you finally got it. I remember, at that time, realizing that I was queer and that I wasn't going to tell anybody. If I told my parents, it would hurt them. They were nothing but good to me, so why would I do anything to hurt them?

A lot of it, too, when you are closeted and sheltered, you don't know the other people that are gay, so you spend a lot of time alone. I always wished I was born black instead of gay, because then people could say, "There he is; he's black, that's it; like him or not," and I'd have a family that's black.

My parents were the most understanding people--my father, especially. Anybody in the world could talk to him about anything, but do you think I could? Of course not; I would do anything I could not to be bad and not to disappoint them.

I think it's too bad that all children--gay or straight--aren't helped with the process more openly, rather than waiting for them to ask the questions. How do they know the questions to ask? They need to be taught more. It works out pretty well if they're straight, but if they're gay, it doesn't work out, because what little bit they are hearing is focused toward being straight. That's why you see so many people who end up getting married for a year or two, having a child, and then, finally, waking up and realizing this isn't going to work for the rest of their life. Then you have broken marriages and children that have a father or mother that's gay.

I think that young adults need guidance growing up, but if I went to the average person on the street who didn't understand being gay and said, "I think you should talk to your son or your daughter about being gay," they'd say, "Don't even mention that to my son or daughter. I don't want them getting those ideas. I don't want them to be influenced into becoming gay." Well, you don't *influence* someone into becoming gay, but most people don't understand that. It isn't a choice. We're born. Once they really realize that, then there's some hope for them understanding.

Jim

I think I'm going in the right direction, but I'm not sure. Something will come along and tell me what I'm supposed to do. I'm a firm believer that people come into my life to guide me from time to time.

A pivotal experience happened for me three years ago, when I went to one of the memorial marches for Charlie Howard. Charlie Howard was a young gay man who was thrown off a bridge in Bangor by several anti-gay youths and drowned. The year before, I had gone and I hadn't yet come out publicly. I brought my camera and said, "I'm just going to take pictures; I'm not going to be in it." I ended up taking pictures and kind of walking for a little bit, then stepping aside and taking pictures. The next year I went, and I stayed for the service. I remember walking down the street, with cars driving by and people yelling obscenities out the windows. There were about a hundred people there, and we got to the bridge and tossed flowers off as a symbol. Then they had a moment of silence, and I can remember looking down in the water. I could almost hear Charlie's screams, and I just started bawling.

After that, they had a rally in the park. A Reverend spoke, and he was telling about a conversation that he had had with Charlie only a week or two before his death. I guess Charlie was fairly flamboyant. He had asked Charlie, "Why don't you just tone it down a bit, and people won't be so hard on you?" Charlie said, "I can't participate in my own oppression." I didn't hear the rest of the speech. I sat there, and those words just kept ringing in my head.

I got home that day and got to thinking about it. It dawned on me that I was participating in my own oppression by pretending to be someone I'm not. All these people who knew me were saying, "Oh, I don't know any gay people." That's when I made a conscious decision to come out completely, and I went and did my first talk.

It's very difficult for someone to understand that after 23 years of always having that in the back of your head, to finally be able to just express it is such a release. People haven't been able to shut me up since. I have a button with a quote from Ghandi: "It may seem insignificant what you do, but it is most important that you do it."

When I was in the eighth grade, a friend of mine from swim team was a lesbian. Her friend wrote this poem for me. It was: "A little wisp of wind can set my mind on end. Oh, what a gentle breeze...." then something about, "I'll never let your secret out." It was like they knew before I did that I was. I have that poem in my scrapbook to this day. At that time, I looked at it and read it, and it didn't mean anything to me.

I wasn't attracted to my male friends, but I knew that I liked being around men more than I liked being around women. At that time, of course, I didn't know there was a name for it. Later on, you learn the names for it--'fag' and 'queer' and 'fairy' and 'fruit.'

I started to look out and see if there were other people like me. You watch TV, and there's no one like that on TV, and you can't find any books on it; you don't see it in a magazine, and no one talks about it. I didn't really see anyone, even the stereotypical gay people. I knew that a lot of people in the family made jokes about 'fags' and 'fairies,' but there wasn't a lot of exposure to it, so it wasn't something that I did anything about.

I do remember having my first crush. I was totally floored by it. I was confused, because it was with my best friend at the time. We never did anything, and I never said anything, but I was really confused about why I was having these feelings. Part of me felt like this was very wrong, but part of me was saying that there must be something to it, or else I wouldn't be feeling this way.

When I got into high school, I pretty much knew that this is how I was. I was really fortunate there, in that I had friends who were gay and very open, both men and women. Having these friends was just the greatest, because you could go out and do things and be yourself. I can remember going home and having to shut everything down. I felt like I always had to be careful, because you had to play two or three different people. That takes a lot of energy.

For a while we lived in Turkey. That was such an incredible experience. It was like stepping back in time. They didn't have ATM's; they didn't have McDonald's; they didn't have packaged frozen meat.

I had explored who I was, and now here I was in this other world. We were there almost two years, and the first year was really good. It was a Department of Defense school, so these kids were all military dependents. My graduating class had ten people in it, so you knew everyone, and everyone did everything together. You fooled around, and you could joke with your male friend and put your arm around him, and you didn't think anything of it, because the culture was that way. Men walked arm in arm and kissed when they greeted each other. That helped me open up some doors.

I didn't come out to my family until I was eighteen, and I was a senior in high school and really rebellious. Things weren't going well, and I came out in the wrong way. I came out to hurt my parents and say, "Ok, I've had enough, so here you go. I'm going to tell you this, and you're going to be devastated for a little while." It was the wrong way to do it, and it was very difficult. It took me fifteen minutes just to say those two words: "I'm gay." I sat there, and the tears were coming down out of my eyes, and I would go, "I...I...I..." I think probably my mother knew what I was going to say, but she wanted to hear me say it, I guess. When I said it, the response was: "Well, we suspected."

When I grew up and started to come out, I didn't know very many gay people. My network was so small, I expected that I had to like every gay person, just because they were gay. Then I realized that there are some gay people I just don't like. It has nothing to do with their sexual orientation. They're just real stupid people.

I think it's important for people to realize that one's sexual orientation is not the only aspect of their life. There's career, family, friends, spirituality, and all of that is intertwined. People have a very narrow stereotype of what gay people are. Because they subscribe to that stereotype, they limit themselves to what they see. I used to deal with a lot of that in my own homophobia, and I still work on it. It's not something that just straight people work on.

In describing sexual orientation, there's a continuum. I always describe myself as on one end. I've always known that I was homosexual. I don't ever recall having dreams about women.

I don't ever recall having fantasy thoughts or sexual thoughts about women. I can't imagine it. To me, it was always a natural thing. It was just a matter of finding someone or something to validate it.

I realize that a heterosexual person may not be able to even fathom why I would be intimately interested in someone of the same sex. I try to explain that I can't imagine what it would be like to be attracted to someone of the opposite sex. I've tried to think about it, but I just can't imagine it.

Sexual orientation is something that shouldn't be brushed under the table and not discussed. If you look at it, what is the issue? The issue is society's insecurity with it and fear of the unknown. You get frustrated, because you think, why do I have to constantly defend against all these myths and lies that have been perpetrated by radically hateful people?

There is a kid who came in to our youth group. When he came out to his parents, who are affluent, religious, upper middle class people, his father said, "When you commit suicide, I'll help you." All I wanted to do was throw my arms around this kid and say, "There are people who do care about you." No matter how bad things may have gotten in my childhood, I cannot imagine having my parent offer to help me commit suicide. Something's wrong here. Something is terribly wrong, and no one wants to talk about it. People want to talk about "family values." I want to talk about those family values that went wrong.

I've come to think of parents dealing with discovering that their child is gay as a mourning, a grieving process. I understand parents having difficulty with that, because from the day they find out they're pregnant, they start developing this child's life: the plans, the dreams, the expectations. When the child is born, they wrap them either in a blue blanket or a pink blanket. We start the socialization process right from the beginning. Then all of a sudden, you find that this child is not what you thought they were. You have to grieve the loss of the person in your mind. I think it's a very natural process, but we need to get them to understand that the image they had was in their mind, not in reality, and that this is the same *person*.

A Gull's Cry...

The Sea came to visit.
I walked between weathered rocks, silent greens,
Salt crusted shores...
Listening to the Wind whisper.

Mist...formed as dew...seeming far off
Yet only inches away.

I sat and stared into the eternal depth
Of a different time.
Seeing our own "Fog Castle."

I taste of salt.
Have I stayed too long...
I feel this chill deeply?

You've touched my soul
Now I drift.
Drift along lonesome shores
Thinking of the gull's lonely cry.

Have you ever heard the song
Of the lonely gull?
Your warmth now gone
I share this emptiness with the song of the gull.
A song only sung when the sea comes to visit.

-- *Gordon Barker*

PART 2

Harry
Virginia
Jay and Dave
Helen and Margaret
Al
Karen
Wayne
Alice
Paul and Gene

Harry

I was never particularly secretive about being gay when I was a kid. But even now, one of my parents still ignores it, and the other one is coming along. It's not my problem. It's their problem.

Through school, I was a gay person. I knew a few people who were gay, but you didn't talk about it. In those days, "out" wasn't yet a word. "Out" was half of outhouse; it was half of something else. That definition for "out" didn't exist yet. "Gay" didn't exist in those days, either. In fact, there was no name for it.

I didn't date as such. I had girlfriends that I went places with, and I had men friends (boyfriends, the same age) that I went places with. But I never "dated." There were people I spent more time with than others, and there were certainly women who wanted to have some sort of attachment that I was never interested in.

Every time I would see my grandmother, after I moved away from here, she would say, "When are you going to get married?" Finally, I got the courage, when I was 31 or 2, to say, "Never, and don't ask again." She never asked again.

I had this boyfriend, this man that I lived with for quite a few years, who she liked a lot. They talked and had grand times together. One time we were having this little spat, and Grandmother was in the car, and she said, "Now, you boys stop that fighting." So, we did. That was a great experience.

When I was very young, I suppose I didn't know that there was a difference, but I can remember from my earliest memories what my attractions were. It didn't become a crisis until I was eleven or twelve. I was trying to figure out how I could possibly go on and not get married, and I arrived at the conclusion that the only way I could possibly grow up and not get married was to become a priest. So that was it. It was entirely settled. Then I had the alarming revelation, a few hours later, that, holy shit, a heathen can't become a priest. So the crisis started all over again.

As an adult, I quite consciously divorced myself from the outside world for a while. I withdrew to the ghetto and did nothing that was not gay for two or three years. I just spent all of my time with gay people. I would go to the supermarket and that stuff, but I did not go to anything public during that entire time. I'd do what I had to do, and then I'd withdraw to gatherings of gays or just stay at home in the ghetto. I got a lot of thinking and working done and a lot of reading done.

As gay people, we have no convention. We're not allowed to marry and pair, so we don't have that sociological mechanism there. Probably, if we were valued and respected members of society, we'd all pair off and go watch TV every night and raise our 2.3 cats per household. In a heterosexual relationship, you've got two sets of parents and all of the brothers and sisters, who are putting their two-cents worth in and having a very real effect on how the whole thing works. I've seen that in your society.

Gay people growing up never get to explore the sexual/emotional side of themselves, except furtively, in a dark, remote place. You're always finding yourself in a dark place, shut away from everyone else. You don't hear other people making reference to the same thing so that you pick it up, even as part of

72

someone else's experience or someone else's conversation. Whereas all the time, walking down a corridor in a school, you hear people talking about *their* experiences as you're walking past them, but none of it relates to you. As a result, we have to do some work on taking responsibility for *our* children, and there are many, many of them out there.

I've been involved for the past nine years in the Maine Lesbian/Gay Political Alliance, working to pass a civil rights bill--or to amend the Human Rights bill in the State of Maine--to include sexual orientation. You have to keep working on educating legislators, which is not always the easiest thing to do. You go up to a legislator, you meet them, it's all fine, and then they find out you're queer. They either try to give you a brush-off, or they'll say, "Well, you're not from my district. I don't feel that I should be talking with you about this." When they are from your district, they'll say, "Well, I know you and the people next door are gay, but there aren't really very many gay people in my district."

I had one, who was my representative, say that to me one time. Well, that night I went out in this neighborhood from house to house with a stack of postcards, and I visited people. The next day, he heard from 28 people in his district that he didn't "know" about, and I only scratched the surface. So then he had to change his lie about why he couldn't support the bill. It came down to the fact that he didn't think he could get re-elected if he supported the bill. So, I challenged him on that. Nobody has ever not been re-elected in Maine for voting for the amendment to the Human Rights Act.

We're looking for equal rights--equal protection under the law. If you're from another minority group, you already have that, but we don't. So what I've been doing is organizing in our community, to make people more politically aware. In the rest of the state, I've been talking with people and speaking before groups.

Which brings us around to the topic of "outing." I've been frustrated about that, lately. I've been threatening to "out" some people. Back when outing first started, there was this great hew and cry among conservative elements of the lesbian and gay community, who just thought it was a horrible thing. I really do think that it's no one's business that one of the bag boys over at the Shop 'n' Save is gay. It would serve no purpose to anyone to "out" him. However, there are people in the Legislature who are gay and who have enormous amounts of power and vote against this bill. I think that is a travesty.

We're not asking them to come and march with us. We're asking them to vote "yes," just to acknowledge the fact that it's the right thing to do. Their lack of acknowledgment is so fundamentally dishonest.

Virginia

I went to divinity school, just to talk about God. It had nothing to do with going into the ministry. I was fascinated with religion and spirituality and figured, here's a place that at least, there are going to be other people to talk with about this stuff. I have a faith and use the term God, but that's a loaded term. I prefer "that which is divine." To put it in my mother's words, "God always provides." Mom's right. I know that I'll be taken care of.

I was born and raised in a northwest suburb of Chicago. My father is an educated man with an MBA, and a very hard-working mid-western businessman from Iowa. Mom is from western Illinois. They're both real good midwestern people, the epitome of the American dream with two kids, and my brother was the three-sport jock. I love my family very much, but I feel like my upbringing was about as shallow as the two-dimensional photograph you see of the white middle class suburban WASP family.

A minister and a musician are the two things that I've always wanted to be, but I wouldn't pursue the ministry, because I always felt like I was a deviant. My actions were not as pure as my faith, so I couldn't be a minister.

I always had a boyfriend. I did everything to look good. I did everything that I was supposed to and nothing that I wanted to, except for music. Something was always missing.

I had girlfriends, too, and with them, I had really deep, intense friendships. They were emotionally charged, though I had no physical relationship with them. I was always taught, you have the physical relationships with boys.

When I was in college, I was ready to get married to my fiance, settle down and have kids, teach Sunday school and piano lessons; and when the kids were old enough, I'd deliver mail to keep myself busy and keep my legs looking nice. I was also anorexic and bulimic, but this did not suggest a problem to me. This was how I left the States and went to England to spend my junior year abroad. I had my long hair. I was a sorority girl and was just as wholesome as can be. I brought an American flag with me, pictures of Ronald Reagan and Bob Dole, and I was a born-again Christian.

One of the first people I met when I got there was another American woman. We were lonely and scared, and we were both Americans, so we started palling around. Our friendship got really intense, but I wasn't going to tell her that I had these feelings for her. Then one time, we were in her room. I was lying on the side of her bed, waiting for her to get ready to go out. She stuck her hand out, and I stuck my hand out. She went to pull me up and she just kissed me from nowhere. That is one kiss I will never forget. It was a kiss that I longed for, and it was so tender. For me it was like the opening of Pandora's box. I knew that this was the way that I wanted to be kissed.

It was hell after that, because of my feelings for her, the fact that we had kissed, the fact that I'd kissed a woman. In the meanwhile, I was thinking, "Wait a minute, I'm supposed to be in love with my fiance. What happened to him?"

At the end of my junior year, I went back and I finished up college. I said, "I will date a man one last time." There was a guy that I'd had this wild crush on ever since my freshman year. I knew that if he wasn't going to do it, nobody was. He was available and I was available, so we made a date to go to Homecoming. We didn't even go. We just had wild sex in my dorm room, but at the end I felt, "It's not going to work; forget it." He was really the barometer. So, basically, I threw in the towel and said, "OK, just live with it. Love is love."

I had a friend my first year in divinity school. She was a very formidable figure, my godsend, in that she was the final push to me being true and honest. I'll never forget her saying, "The only thing I require from my friends is that they're honest," but I didn't know how to be honest. I had lied all my life. It was a challenge, because I was having to change everything, just so I could be friends with her. Then, we ended up getting involved.

That summer I went to Greece, and I carried with me my relationship with her. There is this mountain range there that juts out into the Aegean. It's known as Sappho's Profile, and every night, I would go to sleep under it. Every day, I would spend amidst her profile. There was something unearthly drawing me to it. I'm from the Midwest, and I'd never climbed a mountain in my life, but I had to climb this mountain. The ascent up the mountain is a sensation that's difficult to explain. I was bare-breasted, and I was sliding in and out of the sun. It was liberating. I got up to the top of this mountain, and I remember looking out. Everything was little clouds, and it was peaceful. I just sat up there and meditated. I'd never meditated before, but something hit me. I didn't know what it was, but it was big. It felt like my energy totally shifted around, and something was stripped away. I sat there for hours. I finally said, "That sensation is God." For the rest of my time there, in my quiet, personal time, I sat on the beach, I communed with women, and I had that feeling. It was really powerful and beyond my comprehension.

When I came back, I stayed with my friend, only to find out that she wanted to break up with me. She talked about how come I'm not right for her, what's wrong in our relationship, what she needed, and what I couldn't give. I was traumatized.

Then I went back home to come out to my family. It was my sister-in-law's birthday, and I was going out to dinner with my family. I wondered how I was going to come out to them. I wanted to do the mass family gathering and just tell everybody at once.

At dinner my mother starts trying to set me up with the waiter. She says, "Well, he looks like so-and-so at the office. You know, you and so-and-so would get along great. You have so much in common." I said, "Mom, he's an architect. I like architecture; that's all we have in common." I was very angry.

That night, we went home. I stayed at my parents' house, and it was raining. I was sitting in my bathroom smoking. It's pouring down rain, and I'm furious with my mother. I was also furious with myself because I didn't come out to my family. I was watching the storm outside, when literally from nowhere this lightening bolt comes crashing from the sky into our neighbor's yard, slicing down their willow tree, which was as old as their house. I didn't know I had bitten off all my nails; I didn't even feel the cigarette burning my fingers. It was all in slow motion. Even the raindrops were in slow motion. Something lifted me up from sitting, put me in front of the mirror, and made me look at myself. I looked at myself and said, "I have to come out to my mother." Then something carried me into my mother's bedroom. I have to say it was a power beyond me.

My mother woke up and said, "Can't you sleep because of the storm?" I thought, "Which storm?" I said, "Not exactly. I need to talk with you." It was three o'clock in the morning, but she got up and came into my room. She says, "What's wrong?" I said, "Mom, I've really got to talk to you." This was the first time I had ever spoken up for myself. I said, "You did something that really made me mad during dinner. I was really offended by the way you talked about the waiter. I am not interested in dating this guy at the office, and I do not find you humorous; I do not appreciate it, and I'm not interested. I think you know it's been over three years since I've been involved in a relationship with a man, and I think you know what I'm trying to tell you."

I just looked out the window, and she's says, "Are you a lesbian?" I said, "Yes," and a weight was gone. It was great. Then, her first question was, "Have you seen a doctor?" I was like, "Ok, breathe, Virginia, breathe." I said, "I'm in therapy, but not because of my sexuality. It's because of having to rebel against it, be quiet and hide from it, and tell all these lies. That has really created turbulence in my soul. That's why I'm in therapy." Her next question was, "Are you the boy or the girl?" I wanted to scream, "What a stupid question!" but I ended up saying, "That thought's from the old school, Mom. It's not a matter of being a boy or a girl. It's a matter of love, and it just so happens that the people I find myself engaged with, where my soul meets and merges, are women."

Then I became a wreck. I told her I was going through a break-up with my girlfriend. She became supportive, because here was her daughter crying about the fact that she's going through a break-up with love. She gave me a lot of support. We stayed up for three hours, and I told her everything. It was great.

That morning I went back into Chicago and wrote a paper for school called "Chameleon." It was about the ethics and etiquette of my family dynamic. I talked about how I can't even tell them I smoke, so how can I tell them I'm involved with women. Two days later, I dropped this paper off at my brother and sister-in-law's house. Basically, I came out to them through that paper. I talked with them later, and my brother took me out to lunch. It was classic. He says, "Well, you know what? I don't think you're very happy." I said, "I'm going through a break-up. How do you expect me to be happy?" It was incredible.

So, I was out to three of the four members of my immediate family. I didn't come out to my dad until a year after. He was going through so much at the time. He was working and not working, getting money and not getting money. They were going to sell the house; they were not going to sell the house. It was very difficult, so I ended up not telling him for the longest time, until I got involved in a very passionate relationship with another woman and broke up. I was a wreck.

My father did the standard, "If it's a true friendship, it will last." After two months of crying on the phone to them, I finally just said, "Dad, I really didn't want to do this on the phone, but I've got to tell you. She's more than just a friend. She's my lover." So basically I told him the story. He's a quiet man, and he listened. After about 45 minutes, he said, "Well, I'm attracted to women." I said, "Well, Pop, so am I." There was a dramatic pause. Then he said, "Well, as long as we're not going after the same one, I guess there's not a problem." I'm thinking, this man is too cool; he's not coping.

So, two days later I call back for a follow-up conversation. I said, "Well, Dad, I know we had this great conversation. It was emotional and stirring, but I just wanted to re-visit it to see how you were doing." This time he talked for 45 minutes. To sum up that conversation, he didn't want anybody to reject me or hurt me. I said, "The only thing that would hurt would be the disapproval and rejection of my family." I was wondering if that was what he was struggling with, but he never really said anything about that or showed any emotion. It wasn't so much an issue for him as it was for Mom.

After I came out to my father, I decided to go into the ministry. That was the last of the lies. Everyone who needed to know now knew, and I realized that I was a good person. This is something that I'd wanted since I was eight. I've got to do it. So here I am, I have a year left of school, and I'm loving it.

Jay and Dave

Jay: Of all my relationships, Dave and I get along the best. We like a lot of the same things: we like cartoons, and we're collecting all the Disney movies and the "I Love Lucy" series. We're kind of couch potatoes. For us a good evening is to cuddle up on the couch and watch a movie with a glass of wine. When we do go out, we'll go play cards.

I've had a hard time being in the gay society, because I grew up in a very traditional family. When you met someone, it was for life, and that's what I want.

Dave: That's the way my family was, too.

Jay: When I started seeing Dave, it had been a year and a half since I'd been with anyone. Before that, it was someone I'd been with for years. I wasn't into casual sex. I wanted a relationship.

Something we both agree on is that sex is a small part of a relationship. It takes 5 minutes, 20 minutes, or an hour of the day. You've got to deal with this person 23 and a half hours more that day.

Dave: If one of us has a problem about something, a lot of times, we won't say anything right away. We both develop an attitude first. "What's wrong?" "Nothing." Then we always talk it out. It's really good, because communication is the whole thing. If I'm mad at him about something, if he doesn't know what it is I'm mad about, how is it going to get resolved?

****

Jay: I've always known that I was gay. During childhood, I was always attracted to the male sex, but I always avoided it, because I knew it was wrong. In our society, it's drilled into your head: that's wrong; you don't do that. I was 21 when I finally decided to deal with it.

As far back as I can remember, I've always had a girlfriend. I had sex with my girlfriend, but I was pushing away what I felt. We had gotten engaged to be married, and we'd gone through all the counseling you have to go through. About a month before the wedding, she backed out of it. At the time, I was heart-broken, because I loved her. Now I thank her for what she did, because eventually, I'd have come out to who I am. I couldn't have spent my entire life miserable.

Dave: For years, I had that struggle, and the minute I said, "The hell with it, I'm not going to fight this any longer; I'm gay," everything fell in line, and it was, "Ok, now I don't have to deal with that on a daily basis any more."

Jay: Of course, when you first admit it to yourself, then you've got the "How am I going to tell?" question. You're thinking, "Oh, my parents are going to lose it," and you don't want to deal with it. Over time, as you accept yourself more, it gets less and less of a problem, and you don't really care who knows any more.

Dave: I'm still not out to my parents. I know that they know, but it's something that's never discussed, and I'm not ready to tell them yet. I'm the last male heir, so I'm expected to carry on the name. I don't know how they're going to take it.

Jay: It should be a little easier, because they like me.

Dave: Once they know, then I could care less who else knows. I have him, and he's what I want. If somebody else doesn't like me because I'm gay, that's fine. I have friends who like me for who I am, and I have him, and that's all that matters.

Jay: I told him, when he does tell his parents, if they don't accept it, he's still got me to come back to. Eventually, they'll come around.

Dave: All of us kids have always been very close to our parents, and they have always loved us and done for us. I'm afraid if they take it wrong, and it's, "Get out of my life," that's going to be a crushing blow.

Jay: My father died five years ago, and I'm living with my mother now. She had a stroke about a year ago. She has no short-term memory any more, which makes it really hard, so I'm staying with her, and I'll stay with her until she dies, watching out over her. We're both living there with her. .

She doesn't admit to herself that I'm gay. She knows. I came out to them in '85, which was a battle. I was 22. I'd just graduated from college, and I was in a relationship with a man. My father really didn't say a whole lot to me, but my mother went right off the deep end and was really upset. She didn't want me around the house, because she was taking care of my sister's little boys, and she didn't want to have to worry about them. It was a big, nasty battle. I was asking her things like, "If I was straight, would you worry about me around my nieces, because if I'm going to bother kids, I'm going to bother kids."

Her biggest problem is all she knows and is willing to listen to and believe is what she's hearing in the media, which is all negative. She chooses not to look at me and who I am. She doesn't want to hear it, because what she hears in the news is what gay people are like, and that's all there is to it.

She knows that my friends are gay, which she's not real happy about, but she doesn't admit to herself or anyone else that I'm gay. When we start talking about homosexuality, I'm not part of that conversation. It's my friends or "those people," which, I guess, is her way of coping with it.

****

Dave: I have honestly worked harder than other people, and I think it's because I always thought that to gain everybody's acceptance, I had to do extra, so that I would be liked and I wouldn't feel different.

Jay: You overcompensate to shift the way people look at you. You redirect their line of thought towards the work rather than you. I've gone down a bumpy road, and I'm a survivor. You have to be when you're gay, because if you're not, society will bring you down.

As a couple, you're together, but you're separate because society won't deal with you. That really puts a strain on the relationship. It would be good to be able to go to work and be able to talk about your life, instead of having to talk around it. I would like to see equal rights for us; I would like to be able to have legal, institutional marriages; and I would like to be able to walk down the street and hold his hand and not wonder if someone's going to catch me up the side of the head with a brick.

Helen and Margaret

Helen: My son lives with us, but he regularly goes over to his dad's.

Margaret: He spends every Wednesday night, every Friday night and every other weekend with his father, but this is what he considers home.

Helen: He's eleven. Margaret is part of his family. He says he has two moms, and he has a father and a half-brother. That's his family. In school, when he draws pictures, it's me and Margaret, his father and his step-mother, him and his half-brother, and all the pets.

Margaret: A few months ago, he said something about "queers". I looked at Helen after he had left and said, "You know, I think we're creating a monster here, because that's the only group we never speak of." We never make a big deal about it when we see anti-gay people on TV. We just keep quiet.

When we see things on TV prejudiced against Jewish people or Blacks, we always comment, but whenever a gay thing came on, we'd say nothing. I think it was because we didn't want to be viewed as indoctrinating him, but I didn't hesitate to stand up quite adamantly for every other minority in the world.

So now, we're making an effort to speak about it when it's on TV, like we would about any other group, and he's obviously changed his view. He hadn't really thought it was bad, but he was getting into that adolescent thing of "they're all fags."

He's never come out and asked about our relationship, and we've never come out and told him, but he and his mother have a wonderful, open relationship. They talk about sex and anything else that needs to be talked about.

Helen: He came close the other night. I thought it was going to happen.

Margaret: Barbara Walters was on, and she interviewed Garth Brooks. We all watched it. Garth Brooks has this record that more or less says, "Let everybody be who they want to be." Barbara Walters said to him, "Well, did you think of gays when you were saying that?" He said, "Yes, actually, it's not any secret, my sister's a lesbian. I love my sister, and I think anybody can love whoever they want to."

Paul watched that. Then they went on to Sharon Stone, and they asked her about "Basic Instincts" and the bisexual character. Barbara Walters said, "Does it bother you that people might think you're bisexual?" Sharon basically said the same thing, "I have no problem with it. Whoever anybody wants to love, it's their own business," So, we were inundated with it.

He was sitting there. Helen was ironing and I'm looking out of the corner of my eye at him, wondering what's he thinking about all this. All of a sudden, he got real quiet, and he was looking at us. I could see him looking at both of us, and Helen said, "What are you doing?" He said, "Oh, I'm thinking and thinking." It was like a lightbulb came on.

Helen: He really had that look like, "Oh, wow! I think I just figured it out."

Margaret: Of course, it's going to be difficult when that all comes out, because I think it's hard for any kid to deal with lots of things that happen, but I think it's going to happen soon. Ever since then, he's been different. He'll kiss Helen, and he'll kiss me. He's starting to treat us more like a couple. He always did, but it's more outwardly so in the last few weeks.

The stuff on TV helped, because he's seen people that he looks up to, like Garth Brooks, saying, "I don't see anything wrong with it," and he's starting to verbalize the things he's been seeing and that we've been talking about.

He has a church influence, too. He goes to church and is an altar boy in the Catholic Church; but he saw something on TV the other day, and he said, "I don't care what the Church says; the Church isn't necessarily always right. I disagree with that; I think people should be able to do what they want to."

That was a whole different arena that I had never introduced him to. I don't know where he got it from, but he saw what the Church's view was. He took that, he took what he was seeing, and he took his own thoughts. Then he put them all together and came out with his own opinion, which I thought was processing a lot.

Helen: I'm happy with the way he's turning out.

Margaret: I think that when he hears his friends saying things, there will be peer pressure. I'm sure he'll have his times of calling people fags. Every kid goes through that, but I think he'll tend to stand up and speak his mind like he does now for other minorities.

Helen: I wonder what his friends think of us.

Margaret: I don't know, but they're always very nice. They never ask anything.

Helen: They accept us as a couple, too, because they know we do everything together. We often think, "If those parents knew that they were sending their kid into a lesbian household, they would die. They would never let them spend the night."

Margaret: When Paul has friends stay over, I sleep in the bedroom with the dog, and Helen sleeps out on the couch. That's a two-fold thing. It has to do with the dog who is not real friendly towards other kids. Plus, you'd want the door open, if there's any problem. I don't need to be the one to introduce the gay lifestyle to other kids' lives. If Paul wants to talk to his friends about it, that's his business; but I don't think I should force them to see it. They're young.

When Paul gets to the age that he knows, then that will be his decision. Some friends he might want to tell, and some friends he might not want to tell, and that's fine. Whatever he chooses to do.

****

Margaret: I was just thinking about the different ages people realize that they're gay, and then the hell some people go through, and other people don't go through anything. When I realized I was gay, it was like it fit, like a pair of comfortable shoes. I never looked back. I knew from the first moment that I actually physically did something. Emotionally, I felt it for like six months before that. I never thought twice. I didn't try to say, "I've got to change myself. This isn't right." I didn't go through any of that. I waited a long time, but once it actually happened, I just said, "Oh, that's the piece of the puzzle that was missing. Now I feel comfortable."

Helen: I think I felt that way too.

Margaret: Maybe it's the age. I was 21. Maybe if I had found somebody when I was fourteen, things would have been different, because I would have not been mature enough or educated enough or out in the world enough to know that this exists and it's all right. That was almost 20 years ago now.

Helen: It took me a marriage to figure out that wasn't the way I wanted to go. I didn't date regularly in high school, but there were the proms and stuff that I went to. Andy and I started seeing each other the summer before I went away to college. I was monogamous with him all through five years of college, and a year later we were married. It was "the right thing" to do. I was away at school having just a wonderful time with these three women that I lived with. Andy was back at home, and when I came home for holidays, he was there. We were together for six or seven years before we got married, but when the priest said whatever he says, "until death do us part," I thought, "Oh, my God, what have I gotten into?"

Then being pregnant with Paul, I can remember laying in bed one night thinking, "I don't need Andy around. I don't need any men around. I can do this myself." It was two years after that we got divorced. It just hit me, all of a sudden, BANG, what the hell am I doing? Even though living a gay life is a very difficult situation to be in sometimes, it's more comfortable for me than being married.

We've talked about what happens if Paul is gay. Actually, if I had a choice, I would have him *not* be gay; but what will be will be, and I won't try to change it. Right now, I think he's heterosexual.

Al

Ever since I was little I can remember being more fascinated with guys than with women. Women and I get along well as friends, but I can tell I am partial to guys.

My sister got in a fight with her husband about that. Her husband said, "I know your brother's gay." My sister hit him over the head with a frying pan. She beat him up, because I'm her favorite. She says, "He is not gay," and she called me up. She says to me, "Well, me and George just had a big fight." I said, "About what?" She says, "You." I said, "What did I do?" She said, "He kept insisting you were gay, and I kept telling him you weren't." I said, "Well, he's right." Then she felt bad. She apologized to him and asked me why I went through my life living that lie. I said, "Because of the way you reacted, hitting him with the frying pan." You never know what's going to come out of our family.

My father didn't accept it at first, but my oldest sister was good about it. She says it's my life. If I'm happy, do whatever makes me happy. My father's better now than he was. Everyone in my family's pretty acceptable.

****

I went to New York, because I was bored. I didn't feel like I had anyone to share my life with. I wanted to be a dancer. That was one of my life ambitions. I'd won a lot of little awards for dancing. I got a couple off-Broadway dancing parts there. They weren't very big, but they were parts. I was happy.

The way I met my lover is I got off the bus in New York, and I was walking down the street with my suitcase. This guy comes up, hits my suitcase, knocks it all over the street, and he starts walking off. "I don't know where you was raised," I said, "but anyone that knocks over anyone's shit like that would help them pick it up." So he came back and helped me pick it up. Then he apologized and went on his way.

A friend had invited me to dinner that night. He opens the door, and I look in the living room. Who was in the living room, but the one that knocked my suitcase all over the street. It's incredible that out of all those millions of people in New York, George was right there. Tell me that ain't fate.

Being from Maine, I'd never heard of the HIV virus. That's something they didn't talk about up here. In New York I didn't hear of it either, and then all of a sudden this guy I worked with started being out sick a lot. I started bringing him soup and taking care of him. Every day after work, I'd stop at his house on my way home and make his dinner. I'd sit there and talk to him until he ate to make sure that he ate. Every two days I'd make sure he got in the tub and took a shower. It was sad, though, toward the end. He couldn't even walk, so I ended up staying right at his place with him. George didn't like that. He thought I was carrying on an affair, and all I was doing was giving him compassion.

I had two or three other friends in New York who ended up dying. Then I started feeling ill. I was feeling run down all the time. I said, "Well, I'll try to get more sleep," because I was working three jobs and all. I thought I was healthy, because I was with the same lover, and only that one person, for ten years.

Before that, there was only one person in my life. So it wasn't like I was promiscuous.

Then one time at my bookstore job of reading Tarot cards and doing different things with herbs, I was lugging this box out from the back room. I had an epileptic seizure. The next thing I knew, I was waking up in the hospital. I had been passed out that whole time, while the ambulance came and they brought me to the hospital. I guess it was quite a seizure.

I woke up in the hospital, and I said, "How did I get here?" They said, "You passed out at work, and we don't know why." The doctor gave me all these tests, then he said, "Can I ask you a personal question?" I said, "Why not?" and he says, "Have you ever been tested for the HIV virus?" I looked at him, and I said, "No, but I would never have that. I've been with the same person for ten years, and I've never cheated. I've only been with one person before that, so I don't think I'd have that."

But by then I was sort of putting everything together in my mind about how George was gone all the time. I was thinking, "Is he doing something behind my back to make me unsafe?" Then the doctor says, "Well, can I do one?" I said, "Oh, yeah, you can do one. It's better to know than to not know."

I stayed in the hospital three days that time. I got out and went home. George wasn't there. A week went by, and the phone rang. It was the doctor from the hospital. He said, "Al, I'd like to see you." I said, "You'd like to see me? Can't you tell me on the phone?" He said, "No, this is too personal to tell you on the phone." Right there, I sort of knew. I thought, "Oh, my God." I was at work, but I said, "Ok, I'll be right there."

So I got there, and he asked me to go with him to this restaurant. We were sitting there having something to eat, and he goes, "You're the first one I've had to tell this to." I said, "Tell me what? Stop dragging me on. I'm sitting here chewing my nails." He said, "Well, your blood test came back. You're positive for the HIV virus. That means you've got it." My fork dropped. I was like, "Now, how could I have gotten that? The only thing I've been doing is with one person, and I gave a few people health care, but other than that, nothing."

So, that was the day everything hit the fan. I went back to work and I told my boss, "I can't work the rest of the day. I just got bad news, and I'd like to go home and let it absorb into me." So I went home early. George was sitting there. I look at him, and he's as white as that snow out there. I said, "Oh, my God, are you sick?" He said, "No." I said, "What's wrong with you?" Then I started looking around, and one of his sleeves was up. I should have known right away. I said, "Why's your sleeve up?" I looked on the floor and I saw the needle. Oh, didn't I freak out. I said, "Whether you know it or not, you have murdered me, without even thinking about it, because I just got the results back from my doctor, and I have the HIV virus, and I bet it's you that gave it to me." I didn't catch him with the needle in his arm, but I knew. So I said, "I insist you get out," and I threw him out.

I never had sex with anyone after I found out. As soon as I found out I had the virus, my sex life was gone. I have never done anything since with anyone, and I don't intend to, unless I can find someone I'd be happy with for a couple years that has the same condition; then that would be fine. Sex has never been a big part of my life, anyway.

George died, but he didn't die from the virus. He died from a speedball overdose, which is cocaine and heroin mixed together. It was probably on purpose, knowing him, because he tried a couple other times after I booted him out. He tried to make me feel guilty, but I wasn't in the mood. He killed me, what more could he do to me? I wasn't in the mood.

Now, my doctor won't let me work any more, and I'm bored to tears, so I do a lot of charity work to keep my time occupied. Some people ask me where I get the energy to do things. I just say, "Well, when you lose that energy, you've lost the battle." I ain't afraid of dying. I just know I'll miss my family. They'll miss me, too, but everyone's got to die sometime.

(Al died at 7:50 A.M. November 18, 1994)

Karen

I teach science to non-majors at a community college. I don't do research any more. In a two-year college, you don't do that. Sometimes I miss it. I used to work with electron microscopes, and when you do something like that for fifteen years, it changes the way you look at the world. I look at a leaf, and it's not just a leaf. A lot of the things we know about--not just the diversity of life, but the unity of life as well, like the pattern of microtubules in a cilia--are fun to think about.

Right now I'm feeling like I need to get tenure, but part of me feels like I want to move back out west. My soul is really out there. I've got to decide pretty soon what to do. Professionally, I've been mostly just trying to survive, so I haven't really had the luxury of thinking ahead. I figure I came out as a lesbian when I was 30, I got sober when I was 40, and I'll be 50 next year. I can't wait to see what I'll do.

Development as a woman and development as a scientist can pull a person apart. Development as a young man and as a scientist reinforces each other. It's easy to see the bias in biology and biological research, in terms of the research that's done, the questions that are asked, the things that get funded, who gets to go to graduate school, and how they're treated in graduate school.

One of the feminist critiques of science is that it really has replaced religion as a way of explaining the world to us in our culture and that knowledge is held in a different elite. It's not the clergy in the monasteries any more, but it's the Ph.D.'s and the universities and the government granting institutions that decide what research gets done. It's all peer reviewed, and most of the peers are white males.

It's not as easy to see it in math, but it's there, and that's part of the problem in math education, starting from first grade. Even the girls who do do it--like myself, and I was really good at it--feel weird about it. When I was in high school and got these standardized test scores back and was off the chart for girls, I felt strange. I guess being a lesbian wasn't as strange as being good at math.

****

After college, I was in a Ph.D. program at Stanford. I met a man in California that I married. Actually, I got pregnant. I was 25 years old, and I was sick of being a virgin. He's the only man I've ever slept with, and I got pregnant the second time I did. I never should have gotten pregnant. My period was due, so I figured it was safe. Not true.

In January of 1970, two weeks after Ronald Reagan had signed the most liberal abortion bill in the country, I went to the doctor. The doctor knew I was a grad student at Stanford and offered to arrange an abortion. I knew that Howard didn't want it, and I had worked in surgical pathology in the sixties. Part of my job had been to pick out little pieces of fetal tissue from the placental and uterine tissue from D and C's. That, together with being a good Catholic girl at that time, I just couldn't do it.

So I dropped out of Stanford. That's something that's caused me depression for years and years. I had this four-year free ride in a Ph.D. program at Stanford, but I dropped out, because Howard was in Canada. In 24 hours, I dropped everything, moved, and got married.

He had a one-year appointment up in Ontario and was half way through that. I moved up there in February. Moving from the San Francisco Bay area to Ontario, getting off the plane with this thin little California coat was awful. Oh! That was grim. He didn't have many friends. He was teaching and playing bridge, and that's what he did. That's what he kept doing. And I was just gestating. I couldn't get a job, because I didn't have a work permit, and I knew we'd be leaving in six months. I had good medical care, and I used to walk a lot. We moved to the east coast when I was eight and a half months pregnant, and I had a baby right away.

I started back to school, though. Howard's always been very supportive, but I was very depressed. The second baby was an accident, too. I was trying hard to be a good mother. I look at pictures that were taken then of me with these little kids, and I just think, that's really me? I can't believe I really did that. I was in a state of denial the whole time. I was really trying hard to do it right, but my heart wasn't in it. I never really wanted to have kids. I didn't even want to be married. I got married, because I got pregnant. The way I look at it now is these two children were just meant to be born.

I remember confronting Howard way before I got glimmerings that I wanted to leave him or even that I was a lesbian. I was very unhappy with our relationship, because there just wasn't anything much there.

When my kids were a year and a half and three, we spent the summer out at the coast. I decided to leave him that summer. I was really sick. I had a bad kidney infection. Howard was writing a book, and that's what he did. He didn't know how to take care of me. The doctors in that area were not taking care of me. I thought I was going to die. I really did. My grandfather died that summer, too. It was a really horrible summer.

The Watergate hearings were going on, and my whole life revolved around feeding the kids, taking them for a walk, and putting them down before the afternoon hearings. I just remember walking with these two little toddlers on the promenade along the beach, thinking when they get in school, I'm going to leave him. So I tucked it away and actually left him a little bit before that.

I met another woman, because our kids were together in nursery school, and we bought a house with each other. This woman was married to an Irish Catholic guy, who didn't want a divorce either. Mostly what we had in common was coming out together and talking about our problems with our husbands. I went straight from Howard's house to this place with this woman, and I stayed there four years, until she kicked me out because of my drinking. I was really mad then, but I don't blame her now.

Howard's a good Catholic, and he hasn't remarried. He had the marriage annulled, and I cooperated totally with that. I went down and was interviewed by this nun. I didn't come out to her or anything, but I told her I was an alcoholic, and I said, "I want out of this marriage. It's not Howard's fault. I want nothing to do with the social, political, or religious part of married life, period. I want no more kids; I've had a tubal ligation." So they gave him his annulment, but we're still raising the kids together. We work on it together, probably as much as we would have ever done if we'd stayed together. My kids are now almost 21 and 22.

Wayne

Where I work, at a hospital pharmacy, there's one other gay person. Her lover works in another department. Everybody knows they're gay, and nobody cares. This woman knows I'm gay, because I've told her, and I've told a couple other people that I thought already knew. I've been trying to put things into my conversation a little more. I don't date any women, and I don't go out of my way to say, "Oh, what a babe she is." I try to be me, and little by little, I think they're all figuring it out. It's such a good feeling.

There were three boys and three girls in my family. All three sons in my family are gay. My parents don't say anything. They deal with it.

We haven't told my grandparents we're gay. I think it's fear of upsetting them or fear of being rejected. We should give them more credit, I guess. I have a lot of respect for my grandmother. She's intelligent and witty, and it's almost denying a part of my life, not sharing that part of me with this person who means so much to me. They probably already have figured it out, but we grew up in a family, where if there's something you can ignore, then you ignore it. You just keep up the performance of what they think you are.

Right now, I'm picturing going for a walk through the field and down into the woods with my grandmother, just sort of mentioning this, and picturing how she would deal with it. I can sit here thinking about the excuses I may have, and one of them is that I would be dumping this on her and that she would just worry. It may be that she's been worrying, because I haven't told her in all this time, and maybe it's like the truth will release her. Sexuality is a big part of your life, but it's a small part of who you are.

It took me a long time to become comfortable with the fact of being gay. Growing up gay isn't any easier when you have brothers who are gay, because you still have to accept it yourself, and they were having an even worse time.

Around sixth or seventh grade, I started realizing things were different. You realize that you're watching the crotches of the male teachers, and you feel really uncomfortable sexually, but you still have the girlfriends, and you go to the prom.

There are always the boys that are the woosies and the nerds--the kind that look like victims. That was me. So the boys that are the trouble-causers pick on you, catch up with you after school and punch you out. There is conflict from the moment you hit puberty until the moment you get through high school.

The pressures are there for all the kids, but when everything's pointing to heterosexual things, and you're a gay kid, it's just conflict all the way. When you go to a school dance, you'd rather go with a boy, and everybody else is going with girls. I guess everybody just assumed that all these kids would grow up straight.

Then I started noticing things in newspapers and magazines. Anything that mentioned homosexuality or gay, I would read and just devour. I thought, this is my only connection to the outside world of who I may be. I remember back in '77, '78, there was a kid in Rhode Island, who was a senior in high school, who told the school he was bringing his boyfriend to the prom, and he made national news. I even called information to get his number and called up and said, "Gee, that's really great what you did." That was all I said, but I wanted to do that.

I think I knew that my brothers were gay before they knew I was. When I was a junior in high school, a man from New York had moved up to our area and had started this gay men's group that met once a month or a couple times a month. As juniors in high school, both my twin brother and I showed up at the same meeting. We didn't look at each other the whole meeting. He had a car, but I didn't, and I was hitchhiking home. He picked me up, and he said, "I didn't know." I said, "I knew." We really didn't talk much about it after that. I guess we were still sort of embarrassed, and we weren't a real communicating type of family, even when we knew we had something in common.

I wish they would include other sexual orientations in health class, like it's just a normal part of life. This is as natural a sexual orientation as being heterosexual. Nobody who is straight is going to be converted to gay. That's bullshit. It's like somebody could try to push me into being heterosexual. No way. If somebody says, "Oh, you just made the choice," I'd say, "Yeah, like I would choose a lifestyle in which I could get beaten up, I could get discriminated against for housing and a job, that people are calling me sick. Yeah, I really want to choose that over being heterosexual, which is just the norm." It holds no water.

A lot of people focus on what we do, rather than who we are. I mean, if we didn't have sex with somebody of the same sex, that would make us not gay? It's physical *and* emotional. They think that if a straight man is bunked up in some ship out in the ocean with a gay man that the gay man is going to come on to him.

Look, we're gay; we're not desperate. We're trying to meet other gay men. We don't want straight men.

You'd be surprised, though, at how many married men around this city are out screwing around with other guys behind their wives' backs. If these women only knew. After a while, I started thinking, "Why should I be a participant in letting them be this dishonest?" I made up my mind that I would not have anything to do with anyone that was married. The poor women in these marriages with these husbands that are cheating on them, but I think society's a big part of that. It's very accepted that they're in this heterosexual marriage.

You most likely are working with somebody that's gay, and you don't even know it. I think part of the problem is it's not visible. You don't have to tell your parents you're black, but you do usually have to tell them you're gay. It's really hard when you're invisible.

I read a letter in "Dear Abby" today. This person was writing about how sexual orientation is such a small part of a life. We all go to work. We all drive a car. We all do this and that. It was this big list of things, and by the time you got to the end of it, it just said, "but I sleep with somebody of the same sex." It painted such a nice picture of how similar we all are.

Alice

I knew that I was gay when I was in the sixth grade. When all the other little girls were falling in love with little boys, I was infatuated with a little girl. I didn't understand that at first. I didn't know what being gay was. The word wasn't even a word to me at that point of my life. No one talked about it, for sure. It was something that was so shrouded in secrecy that you just knew whatever it was, it was bad.

When I became infatuated with this little girl, it just happened. I had hit puberty, and I was responding from those emotional feelings. At first, I didn't think anything of it, but then one day it just hit me like, "What does this mean? This is wrong. I'm really bad for feeling like this." That's when I decided that I could never respond to those feelings again.

I remember talking to my mother--it's so clear to me, I can picture it in my mind. I was upstairs in my bedroom, struggling with this terrible feeling that I was such a bad person, because I loved this girl. I called my mom up to speak with me, and I said, "Mom, something's wrong with me," and I was crying. She basically said, "Nothing's wrong with you, honey, don't worry about it." But we never talked about it again, until I came out as an adult, and she doesn't remember that. I think she thought it was just a phase, and she never really took it seriously.

For me, that was the beginning of a very difficult time, because it isolated me. I was afraid to be close to any girls, because I thought I might fall in love with them, and then what would happen? In a sense, I did not have any friends. I chose to keep my distance. That was very hard, but it was my internal fear of being found out. It was not just being found out by the world, but to actually acknowledge it to myself. It was like if I fell in love, then I would have to acknowledge that, yes, I'm gay, but if I didn't fall in love, I didn't have to come out to myself.

I fell in love several times, because that's what happens to human beings. You just do. Every time I did, I would chastise myself something terrible: "Why is this happening to me? I can't let this happen."

I tried to date men. I did date men a few times, and I had sexual relationships with men, but I never was in a "relationship." It was all fake. It was all me trying to fit. I knew I didn't fit. I just didn't want to accept why I didn't fit, and I kept trying.

It probably would have continued, except that I went into therapy for some other reasons. My father is an alcoholic, and I wanted to deal with the feelings that I had about being an adult child of an alcoholic. By the grace of God, my therapist was a lesbian. I didn't know that then. In fact, if I had known, I probably would have run a mile away from her. I know that as I went into therapy and was working on issues, the issue that I could not escape was this terrible feeling that I had about myself being gay. It was always on my mind, but I didn't want to acknowledge it. When you start talking about your feelings, though, it's like the pink elephant in the living room. I couldn't not talk about it, because it was such a major mountain for me. I was very lucky, because I had a therapist who was not only a very good therapist, but she also understood what coming out of the closet really meant. That's when I came out of the closet to myself. I acknowledged it, but it was the most painful transition of my life. Being able to say,

"OK, I recognize I'm a lesbian," was like saying I'm this terrible, terrible person, because for years and years, the homophobia had been instilled in me without anyone ever really saying a word.

My idea of a gay woman was someone who wore leather, someone who rode motorcycles--a real hard woman, who was more masculine than feminine. There are women like that that are gay, and that's okay. At the time, though, I thought that if I recognized myself as being gay, then I had to recognize myself as being like them, like the stereotype that society put in my mind. I didn't see myself like that, and that's why it was so confusing.

There are some parts of me that are definitely masculine, and I recognize those parts, and now I accept those parts as part of me. Before I came out, they were something that I wanted to hide and suppress, so I had a lot of gender issues, because I had a lot of feminine feelings and a lot of masculine feelings. Once I was able to come out, I was able to merge all of those, and now I feel so much more complete as a person and so much more comfortable with my identity than I ever did when I was growing up. I like myself today. I don't have a lot of the self-loathing that I experienced for so many years in my life, and that's wonderful.

I remember the time I actually accepted it. I was living alone, and I screamed it out loud, because I had been holding all of this feeling inside. I remember just screaming out, "Dad, I'm sorry, but I have to be who I am." (I'm getting a little choked up thinking about this.) Once I was able to say that, I could let go of it, and it was okay for me to accept it. That's real painful for me to think about.

My father is very homophobic. As part of my coming out, I had to, in my mind, say that I was going to lose my family, because my feeling was that they were so homophobic that if they knew that I was a lesbian, they would disown me. I knew I could never hide from them. I'm very honest with my whole family, and I knew that if I were going to accept it myself, I also had to be willing to tell them.

As it turned out, none of those fears actually came true. My father was very, very homophobic, but he loved me more than his homophobia. After a few months of me trying to accept it myself, I called them on the telephone, and I said, "Mom, I want you and Dad to get on different phones. I want to tell you something together." Of course, they were really nervous then. I just said, "This is something I need to tell both of you together, and if it means that it will separate us, then I'm willing to accept that," and I said, "I'm gay." My mother immediately, without even skipping a beat, comes back and says, "Lots of people are gay, and I love you anyway." It was almost like she must have known it, but she says that she didn't.

My father, on the other hand, was stunned. He didn't say anything. I said, "Dad, what are you thinking?" He goes, "Well, it's difficult, but I love you, Alice."

It's been hard for them to accept it, but there's never been a point where I felt that they were ever going to disown me, and that was incredible, because that was my worst fear.

Now, after so many years, because I have been very honest with them, they're accepting of it. They're still not comfortable with it, but they talk to my partner, and they ask me about her. They recognize that she's my family, and they're willing to accept that. It's not like, "Oh, great, we're glad that you're in this relationship," but it's okay. I feel real fortunate, actually, because my life has not been destroyed. My life has just begun since I came out.

I think my story started out very sad, but actually, it has turned out very good, because I came out to all of my friends. All of them were, "That's all right," and one of them said, "Well, there wasn't a presumption that you were heterosexual. Our friendship wasn't on that basis." I didn't have any gay friends. In fact, I never thought that I knew a gay person. It ended up I knew lots of gay people that I didn't know were gay--mostly acquaintances, though. Most of the people I had considered friends at the time were all straight.

I have much closer friendships now, because I have exposed a part of me that I thought they would reject and they did not. There was always a part of me that was thinking, "Well, if they knew me, they would hate me." I was always trying to bend over backwards to be such a good person, so they would like me. When I was then truthful and honest and they still loved me, it was like those relationships became so much more valuable and meaningful for me. That has been all new to me, because I never had that before, and it's given me so much fulfillment in life.

One thing that has been good in my relationship with my partner is that her mother accepts me as part of the family, and she makes that very clear to me. That has been a wonderful thing, because it has helped in keeping our relationship together. Part of staying in a marriage is the relationships that you build. You think twice about getting out of a relationship that you have so much vested in. You not only have your family, but his family and the extended relationships that are dear to you over the years.

When I get upset about my partner's and my relationship, I do think about losing her family as my family, and it makes me think twice, so I stay in it, and then I get over that hump of dissatisfaction that I think even heterosexuals surely have in their relationships. There are doubts, but if there are things that can cement that relationship and keep it together, then you get over those doubts and you re-commit.

In the heterosexual community, I don't think people recognize the pain that gay people have gone through and what homophobia is doing. When people say that it's chosen, give me a break! That shows me that they have no concept whatsoever of the pain that a gay person goes through in recognizing and accepting their own homosexuality.

I could not help but fall in love, and it was always with a woman. Whoever chooses who they're going to fall in love with? It's ridiculous. You don't choose it. All of a sudden, you have this feeling, and you act on it, or in my case, I didn't act on it. I suppressed it every time I fell in love, but it didn't stop the feelings from being there. The feelings were rampant. For someone to say that that was a choice is just absolutely ludicrous. I fought it constantly. It was like, "No! You are not going to feel this way. Stop it!" But I never fell in love with a man, although I have always been around men a lot in my life.

I chose a profession in a male-dominated field, and I have always related well to men. I've just never fallen in love with a man, even men that I like--men that are nice people and who have characteristics that I admire. That's just how it is. I don't know how else to describe it.

What is difficult about being in a relationship in the gay community is that there is very little support for those relationships. There are times when people condemn gay people for being "openly gay." With lifting the ban on gays in the military, people talk about being afraid that they'll be "openly gay." I don't understand what they mean by that. When you're openly heterosexual, that means that you can hold your partner's hand. Occasionally, you see a young man and a young woman on the campus making out in the hallway, but you don't see a mature man and a mature woman making out in the hallway. That's youthful love. You're going to have that among young people. They're going to be blatantly sexual, because they're just exploring it. You see it with young men and young women all the time, and that probably would happen with two young men or two young women, who are expressing and exploring their love for one another, but you're not going to have it between two mature women or two mature men, any more than you have it with heterosexual relationships. They express their love differently. The only reason that it's so blatant now is because it is in protest of being oppressed.

My partner and I do not express any sexual feelings for one another in public. I wouldn't even if I were heterosexual, but I would like to hold my partner's hand. I would like to be able to walk arm-in-arm down the street. It's those little things that reinforce your love for one another, those little endearing things that you do when you love somebody. My partner and I do it occasionally, but we're always looking around to see who's there and who's watching. That puts a strain on the relationship.

I see a lot of young women who are not comfortable being gay. They're out, but they're struggling terribly with that internal homophobia. It is so destructive of our relationships. There were times in the beginning of my partner's and my relationship where I didn't even want her around me, because it was like our relationship was sick. It wasn't until I could accept my own sexuality in a mature way that I didn't have those feelings any more, although every now and then they still pop up.

113

In the gay community, we have more self-doubts and more low self-esteem issues, because we have to deal with the brunt of society's discrimination and homophobia. In order to interact in a healthy, fulfilling relationship, you have to love yourself, so that you can love one another.

Paul and Gene

Paul: I was fifteen when I quit school at the end of eighth grade. I had to wait to be old enough to work in the shoe shop.

Gene: I was an assistant foreman there, and I was married at the time.

He's my first relationship, though, because as far as I'm concerned, even when I was married, I didn't have what you'd call a relationship with her. Not really.

Paul: I saw that when I first met them together in their own surroundings.

Gene: Back then, you marry a girl, you settle down, and you have kids. If you didn't, you was talked about; you was outcasted. I can remember a few guys who were single and talked about, even though they didn't look flaunty. They was dirty, grubby, old farmer guys. Back then, it wasn't considered gay; you was a queer. I had a title and a little respect. Then all of a sudden, people's reactions: "The guy's queer. Did you know that?"

Paul: It was getting a little touchy, because people were thinking it was very odd that him and I would be so close at the shoe shop. You didn't see one without the other.

Gene: There wasn't no daylight between us.

Paul: We used to have these secret codes that we'd meet each other at a certain place type of thing. People were starting to put two and two together. One pay day he said, "I'm leaving.

Today's the day I'm leaving." I said, "Well, you're not going without me."

Gene: The only thing I regretted was leaving the kids, but I had no choice. It was a case of sink or swim. We left with just the clothes on our back. We picked up after work, turned around, and walked out and said nothing to nobody. It was like a normal working day. I took her to work, and I took the kids to the babysitter's. I went on to work, and we got paid. That was it. I gave her my paycheck and left with nothing.

Paul: "Here's my check. I won't be home." Nobody knew. We hadn't planned to leave that certain day.

Gene: I had pressure from her, and it was causing me to drink. I was drinking a case a day. It got so bad, I was drinking at work. I had choices to make. Here I was, leading two lives--trying to be "Mr. Nice Guy" with a home, a couple of kids, and a nice car and trying to have an attachment on the side. I don't see how people can have mistresses on the side and still go home and not have a guilty conscience. Maybe it's me. Maybe I'm old-fashioned.

Paul: I like the old-fashioned you.

Gene: So I had a choice to make--either I want this life or a life with him. I chose the life with him. My wife got the divorce about a year later. She didn't even know where we were when we got the divorce.

Paul: We didn't have an address. We lived on macaroni, butter, and Kool-Aid.

Gene: We traded his stereo in for a 1956 four-door Ford. We lived in the car for about four months, going from parking lot to parking lot or back roads. We didn't have any money. Then he got a job, and we lived in a hotel while he worked. I was quite a while without a job. He worked and supported us. Then we found a two-bedroom apartment, fully furnished--dishes, furniture, bureaus, beds, couches, everything--for $28 a week. We stayed in that apartment for seventeen years.

We've gone through a couple fires in which we've lost everything we've owned. We've had our disputes, and we've gone through our ups and downs.

Paul: During our whole relationship, we only split up for three days once at the beginning. I am proud of our relationship.

****

Gene: When we were living in New Hampshire, the kids would come up and see us on weekends.

Paul: We had the children every chance we could. I believe in that strongly, because of the way I was brought up. They are his children, so we're going to be there for them.

Gene: We always made sure they had clothes and food, and they always had toys. They always had a Christmas at our house.

Paul: They were almost like the children I couldn't have. It was part of him. At one point I wanted to become a woman. I think there's still part of me that feels that I could be. I used to wonder what it would be like to have his child.

Gene: We'd have had 1500 of them.

Paul: No, one; I know what birth control means. I got a dog instead, but I used to wonder. I don't think it would change our attraction for each other. Our soul is as one.

Gene: It wouldn't change. He'd still be him. He used to do drag shows, and I was always there beside him, helped him, encouraged him. He's still the same guy. I knew who I was going home with at the end of the show.

****

Paul: I used to work at the corner store down here part-time, but now I've been on disability for a couple years. I can't sit or stand long in one position.

Gene: He's had three back operations.

Paul: I've got disintegrating discs.

Gene: When he went for his last operation, they asked him if he wanted an HIV test. He said, yes. They told him that he was positive.

Paul: I had blood for all three operations. I'm not saying that that was the cause. I'm not trying to put the blame anywhere, because it ain't going to matter anyways.

Gene: Now, we have to deal with it.

Paul: Gene's had an episode that was not too good. He's had a blood transfusion. He's doing better than what he was. I think the mind plays a large part in it, though, too. If you let yourself get into a dead-end thing, that's the way you're going to feel.

Gene: When he first found out, he called his whole family and got them all together and told them one right after another.

Paul: It was like a family meeting, with everybody there.

Gene: He did well. They were supportive, all except for maybe two at first. One still isn't.

Paul: He's a Jehovah's Witness, and he tells me I can change all this if I become heterosexual. Evidently, he knows something we don't.

Gene: It took me six months to deal with it and to be able to tell my family. Surprisingly, they have been more supportive than I expected.

Paul: His family is totally different. I come from one of nine; we're French, and we're close. I mean, one can't go to the bathroom without somebody else knowing about it. I look around, and I say, "I guess I am really lucky."

Gene: My family's been rejective of my lifestyle since Day One. We lived close to them for eighteen years. I could look out my window and see them visiting the neighbors, and they wouldn't come to our house--my mom, too.

Paul: His family is cold. It's hard for me to adjust to that, because I was brought up totally different. If somebody needed something, even though you're on the outs with them, you were there for them and did what you had to do.

Gene: My family is cold and not just toward me, toward each other. But to his family, I'm one of their sons. When they send me a birthday card, it's "To my son." For an anniversary or a special occasion, it's "To both of my sons."

Paul: We're really fortunate.

Gene: Paul and I can't get no closer. We were already this close before we found out we have AIDS. We have a man-to-man relationship. I will talk to him and tell him things because he's a man. A man knows what a man wants and likes.

Paul: I can't imagine life without him. I am lucky to have him.

Gene: We have good times, good memories. They can't take them away from you. Your house can burn, your pictures can go with them, but your memories are there.

Paul: Especially now, a lot of material things we look at, they're nice to have, but they don't have the meaning they used to have. We've sent people home with carloads.

Gene: I might not feel good, but I look around at people that are worse off than I am.

Paul: We are lucky. We count our blessings.

(Gene died in the winter of 1994-1995.)

Etchings

Silhouettes,
Shadows,
Shades of gray and blue.
You're fading.

My mind wanders over pastures
Of memories past.
Trying to recall why I felt
As I did
For what I thought was real.

The treadmill of time
Has vapored the engravings
I once had.
Shadows, now less acute,
Blend.

A haze of blueness still prevails.
At least I'll always know
That once
Warmth existed.

-- Gordon Barker

PART 3

Walter
Alex
Kate and Marie
Wayne and Brian
Jean
Brad
Mark
Shirley
Buddy and Ron

Walter

I credit my early church years for giving me a spiritual base. I say this, and people sometimes cringe, but it's a part of my makeup. I accepted Christ as *my* personal savior when I was eleven, and I have never regretted that.

I probably knew I was gay when I was thirteen or fourteen, and my coming out wasn't under a lot of pressure. I think my first sexual experience was when I was twelve or thirteen with a cousin, who I don't think is gay. I think he was just sexually interested. So from an early age, I was openly gay and surrounded by a somewhat tolerant group of adults.

I was born and brought up on a potato farm in northern Maine. My parents were brought up during the Depression, and they couldn't have friends and fellow classmates back to the house; so when we came along, my father always told us that he was going to make sure that our home would be open to everybody. From a very early age, we were encouraged to bring home classmates, friends, or anyone who caught our fancy on the way home. My mother wasn't happy unless there were two or three strange faces around our supper table. There was a constant flow of people in and out of the house.

Growing up, we talked about current events, and everyone was made to feel they had a voice in what was going on. The late sixties was such turmoil for American society, and we would discuss the pros and cons of the Vietnam war.

It wasn't until I went to Boston after high school, though, that I realized there is a huge gay community out there. I remember my first drink; I remember my first joint. I remember going to the gay bars and finding them to be huge melting pots of all these sexual people. Of course, the early seventies was a very sexual time for most young people in America.

During those years, I developed a serious drinking problem and finally underwent detox. The first year of my sobriety, I really needed to concentrate on what had brought me to the point of drinking to the excess that I did and try to understand what the problems were. So in 1987, my roommate, Dan, and I moved down to southeastern Massachusetts, and I took a year off from work. That's also when AIDS suddenly came out of the closet.

That year, in the kitchen of my house, we started an AIDS support group. I remember trying to put together a mission statement or something to try to reach out. We basically decided that we would offer counseling or home-cooked meals; we would sit with people; we would do what we could for people with AIDS. At the same time, I took the Buddy training with the Rhode Island AIDS Project. The donations came in, and for about a year, we ran this small non-profit group of volunteers. There were no more than ten of us at any given time.

Also during this period, I lost my father, who I respected a great deal. When I got sober, he was diagnosed with lung cancer. I am convinced now, looking back on my life, that one door does not shut, without another door opening. I know it sounds corny; I know it sounds crazy, but that's reality. The last year and a half of my father's illness, we talked a lot about my gayness. We really never had before, because I had been away from home. I went home for visits, but we never had a chance to sit down and talk. He and my mother came to visit, and they got to know some of the people that I was dealing with who had the virus.

My father was one of those dyed-in-the-wool FDR liberal thinkers, whose motto was, "You give back to society what you take from society," meaning that if society is good to you, you have an obligation to turn around and help someone less fortunate, or when it's your turn to help, you help, no questions asked. You don't continually take, take, take, without giving back.

I remember one really wonderful dinner table. There was my mother and father, Dan, a Catholic priest, another friend, and a couple people with AIDS. Just watching my father taking it all in and just that look on his face that this is what life's all about. All I could imagine him thinking was, "What a wonderful thing to be sitting here with my son and his friends, and they're all gay."

Most gay people want to be in a family unit. I think every adult wants to be in a family unit--whether it be mother, father, sister, brother, lover, boyfriend, close friends--the biblical sense of a family unit. The family unit is whoever cares, loves, supports, nurtures, grows, and is there for the other people.

I think that the reason gay people put so much emphasis on their homes is that the outside world is so cruel, and home is where they feel secure. Most gay people in a relationship just want the acceptance of society. We laugh like you do; we cry like you do; we fight in the kitchen over who's going to do the dishes or the laundry. I think that society needs to realize that same-sex couples are just like anybody else. Breaking up is just as hard. Their long-term commitments with each other are the same--till death do us part--and we get divorced just like anybody else does.

I think that we have to work very closely and very carefully with the school systems on education. AIDS education should start very young, and diverse lifestyles should start very young. I mean, teach a child not to hate, and you'll not have a hateful child. It's very simple. Teach a child tolerance of an ethnic group or of the color of someone's skin, and you'll not have the prejudice that previous generations have had.

I think the next ten years will be the groundwork for us to open up the doors, not only for gays and lesbians, but for everybody who doesn't have a fair share. That's what America's all about. If you give me my fair share, I'll give back tenfold, but treat me as an equal. If you don't treat me as a resourceful human being, my anger's going to come out in a different direction, and anger is never a constructive avenue. I think the message that really needs to be put out there is, let's make sure that the kids growing up today have an idea that there are alternative lifestyles. They don't have to follow them, but they have to be tolerant of them, because tolerance is what makes a nation great.

Alex

I'm really tough in high heels. I can dance for hours and do high kicks. My friends are amazed at the difference in me when I change and put the make-up on. They love to watch me make the transition. They'll say, "Oh, I just saw Lexie," but it takes a while before I can look at myself and see her. Usually, I see her coming out when I'm just about done my eyes. When the nails are on, it's like, whooo, here we go. I'm still the same person; I still have the same morals and the same philosophy on life, but my character expands. I allow my feminine side to take over.

Lexie Love came into being four years ago in November. I had some very creative friends that did female impersonation. We had been out partying and went over to their house, and they started pulling the drag stuff out. There was a Barbra Streisand wig they thought looked good on me. Then, we were bored one night, and one of our friends was having a birthday party at this bar, so we said, "Let's dress up and surprise him." We did it, and that's when Lexie first put on a dress and named herself Lexie.

I enjoy being Alex the next morning after Lexie's been out. My feet hurt, because I've been on those heels, and I can wear comfortable shoes. It doesn't matter what I wear of Alex's, it just seems so masculine. I feel butch. It's really interesting to have both of them in my life and to feel both of them. Something I've just started adding to her character is being soft and sexy. There are a lot of people that do this for sex, but Lexie's not doing this for sex. She does it for entertainment and to extend her creativity.

Lexie's helping me, too, because I'm really shy. If I see a man across the room that I think is handsome, I'll watch him for a little while to look at the eyes and the smile. If all the signs are go, I have the hardest time to bring myself to move over there and pick up a conver-sation, but Lexie will walk right over and not feel any fear or insecurity whatsoever. I'm trying to figure it all out and what it means.

****

I had a wonderful first four years with my grandfather and my great-grandmother--a lot of love and a lot of outdoors, natural living and having fun. My mother was there, but she was working, so I spent most of my time with them. I'm sure it was hard for her to be as young as she was and to have the responsibility of having a child, but she was lucky to have family to look after me.

Then she married and just totally pulled me out of my environment and put me into hers with a man who didn't like me at all, and she felt powerless to protect me. I guess maybe she felt lucky that somebody would have her and me at the same time, so we were both going to have to put up with whatever it was.

He was physically abusive, and I spent most of my childhood living in fear. I wet the bed until I was fourteen. Now, as an adult, I realize that that was a product of the fear that I felt inside of me. I felt very isolated. I used to draw a lot of pictures of birds and nests. I spent a lot of time climbing trees and looking at nests and picking flowers. To this day, I can't go by wildflowers without picking a bouquet.

I remember the first time my stepfather stopped my mother from tucking me in. I was five years old, and it was my bed time. She got up off the couch to come upstairs and tuck me in, and he grabbed her by the arm and pulled her down and said,

"No, he's old enough to go to bed by himself." I will never forget that night--walking up those stairs by myself, feeling so alone, getting on my knees and saying my prayers all by myself and getting into bed. That night was very meaningful to me, because I had already picked up on his vibes, and I knew my life had changed drastically. It was not surrounded with the love and fun I had before. It was lonely. I lived for going to visit my grandfather.

My mother stayed with my stepfather ten years before she divorced him, and he literally nearly killed us. Then she went back to him and went through two more years of it. Two years ago, I exploded for 15 minutes about my pain, and she turned on me totally. That's probably the thing my mother did that hurt me the most. I was 36 years old when she did it, and it made me feel like I just didn't want to live any more.

After three months of trying to communicate with her, she was like, "Well, I don't know if I'll ever be ready to talk to you again." She saw me in the store in the town that we grew up in, looked the other way, and just kept walking like I wasn't there. We'd meet on the road, and she'd just look the other way. She doesn't know she brought me within a hair's breadth of killing myself because of the way she treated me. If she would have hugged me and said, "My poor little boy, I'm so sorry," I could have started to channel and release that.

Beyond what was going on with my mother, I had to deal with being HIV-positive and the loss of a good friend who had just died from AIDS. I felt so alone. I had no one to talk to, no one that loved me. I was actually picturing how I was going to end my life.

Sometimes I say, "What the hell is all this about?" It's like, if you believe in past life, I must have been horrible in my past life for all the pain that I'm going through in this life. I can remember the pain I went through telling people I was close to that I was gay, for fear that they would change. Now I'm experiencing the same thing with the HIV, in trying to tell the people that I work with or that I'm close to. In doing that, you take a chance that somebody's not going to be able to handle it and will pull away from you. It's like, where does it end?

It's a really painful thing to have to be gay in this society. Anybody that thinks that this is something that we choose, YEOW! God, who in their right mind, would choose to go through this pain? I do feel very fortunate to have my sister and her husband in my life, though. They accept and love me unconditionally, and that makes all the difference for me. They understand.

I want to start Lexie Love's Official Gay USO Show and entertain the troops. We are the troops. We're all fighting a war; we're fighting a battle--a battle of acceptance, a battle for dignity. There are so many issues that need to be dealt with, and we need to cleanse and heal ourselves and learn to accept the differences in one another.

Kate and Marie

Kate: It's been surprisingly easy to be in this relationship and to put up with the harassment, the headaches, and the discrimination that sometimes happens. If we can put up with it long enough, maybe the community will see us as people first, instead of as sexual creatures first. I mean, my thought when I meet a straight person is not, "What do they do in bed?" My thought is, "What do they do? What's their thing? Do they eat meat or chicken or tofu; do they have kids; do they do Brownies; do they go roller skating; do they like to be outside?" It's really odd. We've met with a fair amount of headache in the process of coming out as a couple, but in a small town like this, if you hide things, I think it encourages people to think that it's bad, so we both agreed not to hide.

I'm more comfortable in this town now, and maybe it's just because I'm in a more comfortable space for myself. I certainly don't walk down Main Street with a t-shirt that says "Tough Dyke," but we also don't go to events in separate cars. I mean, we live together, we're partners, we wear matching rings, and we're both Caroline's mom. The community sees us more than they ever saw my ex-husband and I. They would see him as a fireman, but usually not me. I was not comfortable being part of that unit, and I never was particularly social with neighbors. Even here in this neighborhood, they called me "that woman," until about two years ago. Now we're "the girls," and it's comfortable and nice.

It's a lot of work, but if people know me, they're going to know my partner and my child, and if they know Kate or Marie, they know that there's a child named Caroline that's at their house. Nobody can be sure, if they didn't know before, which mother she belongs to biologically.

We take it one step at a time. Our step for the moment is next year. There are three teachers for the third grade class, and I thought it would be a good thing for Caroline to have the one that's stern, but a good teacher. I was talking to one of her present teachers and got so brassy as to say, "Well, you know, Caroline does live in a bit of a diverse household. How is that teacher going to handle it?" She looked very thoughtful and then said, "Maybe we need to think about where to place her." I'm sure that third grade teacher is not ready to be attacked by two aggravated lesbians, who are there to find out why their daughter's getting harassed, and I don't want Caroline put through that shame. The kids have seen her with two mothers since early in the first grade, and they're used to Caroline with two mothers.

Marie: All the papers she brings home from school--her drawing papers and stuff like that--she puts, "To Mom M and Mom K." The kids will say, "Caroline, your other mother's here." It doesn't phase any of them. It's like no big deal.

Kate: Maybe if it stays no big deal, there won't be the abuse. Caroline's father has been pretty absent her whole life. When I was pregnant, my then-husband and I talked about whether to have the child or not and made a conscious decision to be parents. Then he sort of evaporated. He was there for functions, but not always. It wasn't in the rules that he be there.

When he was moving out, it wasn't pretty here, but I like to keep the lines of communication open. They weren't always open when I was growing up, and I think that's a real important thing. So we started buying books like *Mommy and Daddy Don't Live Together Any More* to foster self-esteem. The kiddo knows that Mom and Dad both love her, although they don't necessarily love each other.

My ex-husband and I have joint custody, supposedly, although he didn't see her for a while. The only sticking point of the whole divorce was when he made allusions to him getting full custody of Caroline, because I was a lesbian. It just set me off into an absolute twirl. I was very agitated. There were not many things out of that relationship that I was adamant about retaining, but child custody--my child living in my house and being properly parented--was one of them. She's my number one priority, until she's eighteen, nineteen, God help me, thirty-five years old. Some things come first, and you can be a lesbian and a mother, and they are synonymous.

When Caroline's home, I spend time with her. I work second shift, and it's important to me to be a mother. If my friends want to do social things with me, sometimes they have to do it with an eight-year-old tagging along.

Now Marie and I are assistant Brownie leaders for Caroline's Brownie troop. Her leader was just having a hiss, because Caroline had two mothers, because it's not "normal", and "it doesn't fall under the code of Girl Scouts and Brownies." She's a right-wing Republican for whom it's okay to physically and emotionally berate your children, but it's not okay to have two loving gay parents. We went through this kind of tug-of-war, and

135

we'd say, "Yes, Caroline does have two mothers, and yes, that's okay. It's okay for her to talk about it, and don't you dare shame my child, because hell hath no fury like Kate when her kid's been harassed." At the end of all that, there was a *Brownie Leader* magazine, and their feature story a month ago was on diversity. I thought, "Oh-ho, going to frame it. Going to give it to this woman." Brownies and Girl Scouts are much different and far removed from Boy Scouts.

Marie: Boy Scouts is like a fraternity. They're like a loyal order, a fraternal organization.

Kate: Fraternal organization of heterosexual men. If you can't be a gay man and be a Scout leader or a Scout, then you shouldn't get United Way funding. I have a right-wing radical friend, and we get into it hot and heavy on the United Way issue. She's a Boy Scout leader, and I'm a Brownie assistant leader, and she said, "Well, you and Marie are different." I said, "We are not any different than anybody else, and we would no sooner have intimate sexual relations with a *child* than would a Boy Scout leader." We get into these great long debates, but she just doesn't understand.

Wayne and Brian

Brian: I think I'm closer to my brothers and sister now than I was when I was growing up, but I get along better with his family than I do my own.

Wayne: Well, you're out to my family, and you're actually not out to yours.

Brian: No, it's not discussed. We're a Catholic family, and we never really talked about any type of feelings growing up. It just seems natural to me not to discuss relationships. He's gone to some of the family functions, and he's met all my brothers and sisters and my mother. There was five kids, but my younger sister died in a car accident a while ago, so now I have one sister and two brothers.

Wayne: When his younger sister died, that was a tough time for him, but it was also very awkward for me. I didn't go to the funeral, and I didn't really come near to your family, because I didn't know how I was supposed to react to it. That was about five years ago. We had only been together five years at that point. Your parents didn't appear to be as open about it as your mother does now. It was still hidden more from her, and your father was still alive.

I had no idea what I was supposed to do. Should I go to the house? Should I take something over to eat? Should I send a card? I think I did send a card, but I didn't know what my role was, and nobody could tell me. If the in-laws don't know of the spouse, are you supposed to sit in the back, or are you supposed to sit down front with Brian? Are you supposed to take a separate car? I didn't have any idea how to approach the whole thing, so I stayed away from it. I stayed home and took care of Brian when he was home and sent him off when he had to go over to his family's.

Brian: It was a different circumstance when my father died, though, because you went to the funeral, and you were there.

Wayne: I was closer to your mother at that point, and I knew all your brothers and sister better; and your father was dead. He seemed to be one of the major roadblocks between us. Plus, I'd already been through one funeral with you. I decided afterwards how it should have been handled. I felt like I didn't handle it properly, that I didn't have any other choice, but I decided that it was handled wrong. So the next funeral, I had a better idea of what I thought I should do.

Brian: We went over together to the funeral and to the cemetery.

Wayne: But even at the funeral, you and your sister and her husband and your brother and his wife all sat down front with your mother, and I sat in the back. So even that was not the same.

Brian: You were more involved in that one, though, than you were before, but I had to get the support from him mentally, privately, away from the family.

Wayne: Right, and in the funeral and during the service, I had to beam it down to you, whereas your sister's husband was sitting there holding her hand. It just seemed very traumatic to me. I felt totally lost. I didn't know how to present myself, how to act, or how to do anything. I know that it was much more traumatic for you, because you were with your family, but for my

138

part, I felt like a failure, because I didn't know how to handle the situation. What am I doing here? I'm washing your clothes, so you can have something fresh to wear in the morning to go over to your mother's. That was the only way I could contribute.

Brian: His is a closer family. They express their feelings more than my family ever did.

Wayne: I'm the oldest. My brother's two years younger, and I remember playing with neighborhood kids. I was much more social when I was younger than I was when I got into high school. There was a group of kids that used to play together quite often, but I always felt different from them and had different interests. I was not sports interested at all. I was much more interested in homemaking than in the traditional boy things.

We played cowboys and Indians and cops and robbers, but I'd always be the heroine. I tended to be the girl. I always wanted dolls, but I never could have them. Although we did get some dolls, they weren't girl dolls; they were boy dolls: G.I. Joe's, a Joe Namath doll, and some cowboy-style dolls--Jane and Johnny West and their little family of children. My brother got the Johnny, the Jay, and the Jamie West, and I got the Jane, the Janet, and the Josie West--the girls. I'm sure my parents weren't thrilled with the idea, but they knew that's what I wanted, and they let me have them. I think that's why I have such a close relationship with my family now, really.

In grade school, I was usually a one-friend person, but I never felt totally comfortable with kids that liked me. I couldn't really tell them everything. I had something that I had to hide from them. I was going through a stage at that time, where I really was wishing that I had been born a girl. Things would have been a lot simpler, because at that point, I had learned enough and knew enough to know that I was thinking and feeling the things that the girls were thinking and feeling, not things that the boys were. So I felt, then, that something was screwed up.

I kind of withdrew from friends at that point. I just spent time with my brother. My brother and I were our own best friends, but we didn't really talk about those things. It's not something that you feel you can talk about with anybody, even your brother, so I just held it in and dealt with it the only way I could.

My high school years were spent trying to find God, to solve my problem. In my church you got saved, so I was looking to get saved. I should be thinking of girls in this way, not of boys, and try as I may, I couldn't do it. I couldn't make those feelings go away, and I did try. I prayed, and I cried, and it didn't change anything. I decided that the only way to solve this was to find the *correct* religion, because it had to be out there. I investigated a lot of them, but I'm still gay. That's how I spent my high school years, was very religious oriented and trying to live the straight and narrow.

I had a girlfriend who was very religious and went to church four times a week, and I went to church with her. When we weren't in church, we were spending time with her family. I tried so hard that I had, at one point, gone through the motions of becoming 'born again,' so that I could be washed of my sins and start new with Jesus. Nobody tried harder than I did. I had the best reason in the world to go through it, and nobody believed any harder than I did, but the feelings didn't go away.

Brian: In high school I thought I was the only one feeling that way. I think it might have helped if they had mentioned homosexuality as being a normal feeling during a sex education course.

Wayne: Or even acknowledge that it existed. Whether calling it normal or not doesn't matter, just so that you don't think you're the only person in the whole wide world who feels this way.

Brian: But they should say that it's normal. It's the way I was born.

Wayne: My parents had bought us some books to explain sexuality and childbirth and all the stages of the birds and bees. I looked up homosexuality in that and found a paragraph. In a four-book volume, it was one paragraph, and it wasn't positive. That's all I could find.

****

Brian: Why do people "choose" to be gay? Well, we don't choose it. The only thing you choose is to accept who you are. I didn't choose to be gay. I would never choose to be gay--to be persecuted and hated. The only thing I finally did was say, "OK, Brian, this is the way you are. Accept it, and don't try to pretend to be somebody you're not." I tried that in high school. I tried to date and tried to do what everybody else was doing.

Heterosexual people don't realize that gay people have the same type of relationships that they do. They do the same things: they pay their bills, go grocery shopping, repair their house, go on vacation together, and watch Murphy Brown. A lot of people think that gay people are just sexually active and that's it.

Wayne: I think the best thing that I can do as a gay person is just what I'm doing--being myself to everybody.

Brian: I think gay people want people to know that we're just ordinary people making lives for ourselves--regular folk.

It was sort of strange when we went to Provincetown, because we actually walked in the street and held hands. It felt nice, but strange.

Wayne: It felt good to be able to do it, but it felt wrong at the same time. You're stepping out of the way, because this baby carriage is coming at you, and I'm thinking, "Oh, I shouldn't be doing this. There's kids and there's straight people around," but they didn't even look at you twice. They're used to it, and they don't have a problem with it. That's the way it should be everywhere.

Jean

Back in 1981, I attended my first and only Michigan Women's Music Festival--4,000 women all congregating together. I had a wonderful time, but I was a lot different than a lot of those women. First of all, I ate meat. I was going bananas, because it was a vegetarian place. For four days, no meat. It was killing me. I had to finally have somebody take me out, so I could get a burger. It was awful. If you were carnivorous, God forbid Republican--which I am--and liked and appreciated money, there was something very wrong with you. My only saving grace is that I wear Birkenstocks. I do that because I have such small feet that pumps don't fit. We all come in different packages.

My spiritual side is real important to me. It's gotten me through a tremendous amount of stuff in my life. At one point, there was an average of one important person in my life dying a year over an eight-year period. When I was in college, my mother, a cousin, and an aunt that I was very close to all died. If I hadn't had a belief, all that would have been a little too overpowering.

My father knew about me before I knew he knew. He knew before I got married. He had a conversation with my cousin, and he said, "You know, I can't figure out why she's getting married," but I never had a conversation with him about it, ever. Up to the time he died, we never discussed it. I know he really liked my ex-husband a lot. He liked the woman I was with after that. He died while I was with her.

I went all through college dating both men and women and ended up getting married. The guy that I married is an absolutely marvelous guy. I still love him. He knew from our second date that I was bisexual and I'd had girlfriends.

He met me two months after my mother had died. He wasn't my knight in shining armor, but I really needed a good friend at that point, and we were best buddies. His sister used to comment, "You seem like you guys have been together forever. You're not huggy-kissy, but you really love each other." We really did, and we still do. It was strange the way it started, and it might not have ever even progressed if timing had been different. I think it worked for him in a way, and it worked for me in a way.

I married him, because I loved him. It's that simple and that complicated. We had dated for about five years. After we'd been married for only about a year and a half, I met a woman that I was interested in. I didn't plan on living with her, but it really opened my eyes to the fact that I just can't do this. Of all the people that I have been involved with throughout my lifetime, no break-up has ever been harder for me emotionally than that marriage, because he was such a wonderful guy. I'd never planned on having kids, so it wasn't that I was now not going to have children. It was just very difficult. I'm glad that he and I have been able to maintain a friendship.

Then there's Barb, the joy of my life. So far, we have avoided any kind of a commitment service. We've talked about the fact that we'd like to get "married" at some point, but we've both been in relationships where we considered ourselves married to the other people, and we're both gun-shy from that. She has a daughter who keeps saying, "So when are you guys going to get married?" Her daughter considers me a parental unit, which is really neat. She also has a son who's in college, and we hit it off real well. They tell me their mom's happier than they remember ever seeing her, so I take that as a good sign. We work at it.

Work, too, is very interesting at this point in my career. I'm self-employed, and my title is chartered financial consultant. I spend my days making sure people have a way to survive financially in the future, whether it be retirement or funding college for the kids. Most people haven't done a tremendous amount of financial planning, and my main purpose is to focus them. In that process, hopefully, they're interested in the products that I have available for sale--mutual funds, annuities, and insurance products. It's a neat kind of a job, and I've been doing it now for thirteen years.

Two days ago, the State Association had their convention, and I was elected president, which is a really neat thing, because I'm guessing that about four percent of their membership is female. No female in this state has ever gone higher than I have now reached, so I'm really breaking ground here.

I'm not "out" in this city. Some people think it's kind of funny, because a lot of people in town know about me, but it's one thing for them to know; it's another for me to tell them, and I've chosen not to do that. My family is very well known in this area. It's not just me that's going to be affected; it's going to be them, and I haven't wanted to do that. I'm a private person in that regard. I don't flaunt my sexuality. I wouldn't if I was straight. I don't want to make people uncomfortable wherever I am, and I don't want them to make me uncomfortable.

Brad

I think I was kind of a loner, even as a kid. I'd spend a lot of time walking the beach. When I got to be a teenager, I spent more time alone because all of my schoolmates lived in the next town. It was difficult for me to get there, so I never did hang out.

I was involved in after-school activities. I was in the band. I never played basketball, but I was the manager and scorekeeper, just so I could go out to all the games. That was in my early high school years. When I got to be a senior, I got screwed up, so I didn't stay involved in much.

Emotionally, I think the gay issue came out when I was sixteen. I didn't know what it was when I was a little kid, but as I look back, there was definitely something there. I think even as a little kid, I was attracted to men; but I didn't know much about it, and I didn't know anybody else who was.

I dated a girl in high school for a few months. It was probably to prove something, in a way. It was the thing to do. Maybe it was just going along with the crowd.

I also went to church every week and was involved in the church, until the time that the realization of being gay came out. Then I felt like I didn't belong there any more, even though it was a Congregational Church, which isn't really fundamental.

My first gay experience was at seventeen. It was with a cousin, who was almost the same age as me. It wasn't a very good experience, but it was something that once I did it, I couldn't stay away from, because it was there. I think that made me feel like I didn't fit in anywhere, because back then "gay" wasn't really out enough. So there wasn't anyone to talk to about it.

I ended up taking an overdose of Mom's tranquilizers and being rushed to the hospital. I left them a note, so it all came out that way. Even after that, it was never really discussed. My father seemed okay. He's pretty easy-going, but my mother is the hyper type, so she doesn't deal with anything well. She wants things to be just so, and when they're not, she can't deal with it.

I wouldn't go back to those days for money. It was just a real difficult time, adjusting and realizing who I was and feeling like I was the only one in the world, even though I knew I wasn't. I'm not sure what things are like today. I think kids today are becoming more sexually aware a lot younger, so they know more, but society still puts a stigma on being gay.

After high school, I went to college for a year. That was a horror show, because there was no gay group or anything like that at the University. I think I've always been a romantic. I wanted to find the right man, fall in love, and live happily ever after. I would focus on different men, one at a time. These people weren't gay. They were mostly men that were in my dorm that I got to know. Nobody ever really shunned me for it, and people tried to help; but I was pretty screwed up. I hadn't come to terms with it myself, so I really became a pain in the neck to these people, always looking for attention and to talk. That was a difficult time.

The next year, I started working at an Italian restaurant. Then, someone I had known from college the year before got in contact with me and took me to a gay meeting some place in the city. That's when I had my first real taste of "gay." Immediately, I fell in love with someone. It lasted three months. Then there were a lot of years of drinking too much and partying a lot, although I never got into drugs.

When I found out I was HIV-positive, I got bad advice: get rid of all your assets. It cost me quite a bit of money, because I had an IRA which I closed out, so I had to pay the penalties and taxes on that. I went to the extreme. Then I slowly worked my way back to the way everything was before. I can't think of much that I do differently now. Maybe my attitude's different, and I'm not really wild about sex any more; but then I never actually was, when I think about it. I like to be with someone, have the physical contact and the closeness, but to me, sex is just a lot of work.

I'm healthy. I haven't even had a cold this winter. My T-cell count is still above 200, which is a number that they go by, and it's been there ever since I started being tested five or six years ago. It's dropped some but not a lot.

There's still a lot of people out there in denial, who won't get tested and who are having unsafe sex. I worked as a bartender at the gay bar for six months a couple years ago. You still saw the same things going on that went on before AIDS came along. That's kind of scary.

At the restaurant, I work with women. When they meet somebody new or are going out with someone, I come right out and say, "Using a condom?" "Oh, no, he's OK." "How the hell do you know?" They won't listen. There's a lot of denial.

Even after I heard about AIDS, I didn't think too much about protected sex, until I found out I was positive. Everyone thinks they're going to last forever. You think, "Oh, well, I never screwed around as much as so-and-so, and they're okay." Well, I wasn't really sexually active in the four or five years previous to my test, but I did have sex. You don't have to be active, except once.

149

Once in a while, I have a little twinge of fear. It's not so much about dying as about not being able to take care of myself. I would hate that. I'm not good at calling up people and saying, "Can you help me?"

A while ago, I read a concept that we're all part of the universe. Physically, we are, but even after you die, you're still part of it. Death cannot conceivably be an end. There's something after. I'm not sure exactly what, but I firmly believe it's nothing bad. I don't have a big problem from that point of view. There have been so many incidences of the beauty in near death experiences that it can't be bad.

Everybody's going to die sooner or later. Even if you can not cure AIDS, if you have a good attitude, then your passing, or whatever you want to call it, is not going to be that emotionally difficult for you, because you're going to be accepting yourself and everything around you. Whereas people who fight the whole thing and have a bad attitude, they go out more horribly, I think. Maybe there's not much you can do about the actual physical part of it, but a lot of your physical being has to do with your mental being, too, so if you can get that in order, then the rest of it shouldn't be as bad.

Mark

I think people get this idea that just because you are homosexual that you live some wild lifestyle. I get up every morning like everybody else, go to work and come home. I eat my dinner, watch my soap operas, visit with my friends, and go to bed. I don't know what people expect.

My parents taught my sisters, "You just don't jump into bed with a boy because you're feeling frisky or that's what he wants you to do. I'm not saying you have to wait until you're married, but you wait until you know the time is right, and you take responsibility for it." Even though I was a boy, I listened to my parents. I fooled around with guys, but I was 24 when I had sex for the first time with my first lover. To me it was a big deal. People tell me they're 21 and have "slept with 60 people." I wouldn't be bragging about that. That ain't nothing to be proud of; at least not to me. I don't see anything impressive about it.

I was 26 when I came out to my family. I called them all together, and they said, "We've suspected this for years," and it was no big deal. My sisters-in-law and my brothers-in-law are all comfortable. I've been really lucky that way, because I have friends whose parents haven't spoke to them in years, since they found out, and when they do see them, they can't mention the other person in their life. That's too bad. I want to share my life with my family, and they feel the same way. I was relieved. It was like a weight had been lifted off me.

I had a friend about my age. His sister and I were real good friends. He was gay. I knew he was, but we never talked about it. He was probably 24 when he came out to his family one night. They could not accept it. His parents went crazy. They just could not deal with it. He went out and got drunk that night, and I don't know what else he was on, but when he came back, he took the shotgun and blew his head off. His parents heard him come in that night and they just thought he was drunk. He got the gun, then he went out, parked behind the schoolhouse, and shot himself. To this day, they are blaming themselves, because he was still their son. He was still the same person. He was just gay. Neither one of them have been the same since.

I never asked to be gay, and if I could live a straight lifestyle, I would do it. If I had my choice, I'd have a wife and kids right now. I've tried. It just wasn't for me; but it was difficult growing up gay.

I was very young when I became aware that I was gay. I know it seems strange to a lot of people when I say this, but I was only five or six years old. Even that young, I knew the attraction-- not sexual attraction--but I liked the looks of the boys more than I liked the looks of the girls.

What I heard my whole childhood was that I was a sissy, because all my friends were girls. I don't know why, but that's who I always hung with. I would have hung with the guys, but because I hung out with a girl after school, if I wanted to go do something with the guys, "Well, he plays with girls after school, so..." I was just blackballed.

I went to visit my cousin at school for a day when she was in high school. I was standing there, and I got a lunch bag with a full soda can in it in the back of the head because I was queer.

After that, I learned you've always got to be aware of what's going on around you. You never know when someone's going to jump you just because someone said, "He's a sissy, beat him up."

My friend and I went to Portland for a weekend last spring. We were walking up the street in jeans, jean jackets, baseball caps, not doing anything, and this carload of young kids drives by, hollering "faggots" and "queers." We looked at each other and said, "What are we doing? We're not doing anything." An hour later, we were coming back and crossing the street when this guy rides by and yells, "Get the hell out of the road, you faggots." Sometimes I think I've done something to deserve this treatment. I know I haven't, but it makes you stop and think.

****

My first job, I started out as a dishwasher in a restaurant Downeast, but a man had never washed dishes before. That was a woman's job. Women waitressed and did the dishes. A man just didn't do that. When I'd go out front to take the clean dishes out, some of the fishermen that came in for lunch would say "faggot" or, "It ain't right that a man's here washing dishes," and it bothered me. I thought, "What am I doing wrong? I'm earning money to support myself and I'm doing a good job," but it was hard. There would be days I didn't want to go out front with the clean dishes. I'd con the waitresses into taking them out, because I hated being out there with people commenting about me.

Then I started cooking. At first, they didn't want no fag cooking their food. After a while, it was, "Well, make sure Mark gets my order, because I want him to cook it." I cooked there for fourteen years and, not bragging, I turned out to be one of the best cooks they had there.

153

Shirley

As a kid, I had very little, if any, interest in boys. I had slightly more interest in girls, but just for friends. Mostly, I guess I was a loner. I liked to do my art up in my room by myself. I liked to play with my horses out in the barn by myself.

When I was in tenth grade, this boy, who was a senior, started paying attention to me. That turned my life around. All his friends were older, and I got in with this older, fast crowd, and overnight, my whole life was different. Maybe I still didn't have very many friends and nobody who knew me really well, but at least there was some place to go on Friday and Saturday night and someone to hang out with at lunch time at school. He was a nice enough boy, and immediately, I lost my virginity and started smoking dope and getting drunk, all in the same night. From then on until I got out of high school, that's what I did. I don't even know why I had sex with him. It was just the thing to do, and it didn't seem like a big deal. I was really a little slut after a while.

I left high school early. I did all my credits in two years and got out. I got married to this guy. He was nineteen and I was seventeen, and everyone thought that we got married because I was pregnant, but I wasn't.

I don't remember having any sexual feelings about women at all. I remember having intense emotional attachments to some of my girlfriends, but when I got married, I quit having those kinds of girlfriends. We moved away to the Seattle area and got jobs in factories. I just spent that couple years growing up. My husband was a nice guy most of the time. He wasn't physically mean or abusive, but he was a little bit macho, the implication always being that if he wanted to do something to me, he could. We really didn't have anything in common, except we liked booze and drugs. Then we both decided to try going to college.

Basically, what came out of that was a divorce. The community college I was going to was in this working class factory town, and there were a lot of working class dykes there. One of them was a model in one of my art classes, and I just fell flat in love with her. I had no friends--none--and I lived in this little tiny house that I rented, and I had a roommate, who was a straight man and kind of a zero. So I spent the winter reading books about lesbians--the seventies books, the really radical kind of feminist, separatist ideology books.

Then I scared myself so bad that I got back together with my husband, just because I didn't know what else to do. I didn't know where to meet women; I didn't know how to meet women. He didn't care. He said, "You can sleep with whoever you want to; just come back."

I managed to finally break it off with him. Then I met a woman I fell in love with at a bar. That was really intense and fun. She was fourteen years older than me, and she had a lot of money at the time. I had none. She decided to bail out of the culture and become a separatist, so we became separatists.

I was 22, when I finally came out as a lesbian to myself. I don't remember exactly how I came to tell my mother, but she was not happy.

I got sober in '84. I joined AA, because my drinking was really awful. After about a year, I met Karen, my current roommate, there. We've been living here for seven years, and we lived together for a year before that. I haven't ever been in a relationship for this long. I guess somewhere in here I've grown up. Now I'm a responsible adult.

I'm a Jew, and the rest of my family are Born-Again Christians. I decided that I was a Jew when I was ten years old. Even though I dabbled around in feminist spirituality, it never did anything for me, but the religious thing is very real, and my family will not leave it alone. They do better around my being a lesbian than they do around the religion thing. On the other hand, though, what my mother says is, "All you need is a nice Jewish boy."

Most of my friends are really anti-religion. They really hate organized religion. Karen absolutely hates, *hates* me being a Jew. Fundamentalism, Catholicism, and Judaism are all the same to her--*the patriarchy*, or something like that. I'm a practicing, observant person, and she just hates it, so I don't have anybody to really talk about these things with, except for the women in my synagogue.

That's one thing about lesbians that I got really bored with really fast. I guess I'm kind of a reactionary. I found the whole feminist analysis really tedious, boring, irrelevant, and completely useless to me. I'm not an intellectual person. I don't like that kind of stuff. I tried to like it, because I thought it was the right thing to do. I think I'm very educated on it, and I hate it. I'm glad somebody wants to do it, but I don't want to do it myself, and I don't want to live my life governed by that kind of ideology. I think a lot of it's really fairly boring, and that's the nicest I can say about it.

I kind of like moderation, the middle of the road. Sometimes it seems like a cop-out, but I'm thirty-five years old, and I don't want to be a radical any more. I did it for eight years and got really burned out and sick and crazy from it.

I've been an art teacher for six years now. Being a teacher and being a lesbian is really hard. I'd have to say it's the one area of my life I'm not comfortable with. I was never really in the closet before. Even when I was in college, I was not in the closet for anybody who looked closely, but I'm in the closet at work, and I'm very conscious of it all the time. There's no alternative, and I think that it does have an effect on me.

I'm thinking now that I would like to stop teaching within five to ten years. I can't see myself doing this my whole life. It feels so dishonest, and I don't think that anybody is doing the kids any favors by protecting them from the fact that they know a queer. Every single one of my students will swear that they've never met a queer and that none of them are going to be one, either. It's so wrong. It's bad for everybody, and sometimes it effects my self-esteem.

Buddy and Ron

Buddy: Ron's helped me a lot dealing with the guilt of being gay. I've found myself, and it feels good not to have that burden. I don't run around telling everybody I'm gay, but if they know, fine. I have four secretaries and five other staff in my office, and they all know, but it's not a topic of conversation. There are some that can't deal with it, and that's too bad.

I'm happy for once in my life. I always had the facade of being happy-go-lucky, but now I'm content and I'm happy. I'm happy with me. I'm happy with us. I've finally found myself, and I'm not a bad person. I used to think I was. I guess I can say I'm proud to be gay.

We're at the point, now, that we depend on each other. We're totally in love with each other. I loved my wife, but I don't know if I was ever *in* love with her. I've found my life partner now, and it feels real good. We spend our time getting to know each other as a couple, and we do a lot with my sons.

Ron: We've had some arguments about the kids.

Buddy: Yeah, I ignore him. I get the boys what they want, even though I may be strapped at the time, because I don't want them to think of me the way I felt about my father. If I have to say no, it hurts me deeply. I feel as a father, I can't do too much for them.

Ron: They're spoiled. Buddy makes a decent salary, and his ex-wife makes a decent salary, so whatever the boys want, the boys get. Me growing up with eight kids, you didn't get what you

159

wanted. You got what was affordable, if that. When I moved in here, I started getting on him about it. I was like, "This is our life now. These are your children, and you don't have to buy them everything they want. We can't afford it."

Buddy: I came to the realization, too, that maybe I was doing it out of guilt because I left them. Financially, I do make a good salary, and my ex-wife makes a good salary. With everything we're going through right now, things are changing. I'm basically taking care of two households.

Ron: I don't mind the kids coming over here on their every other weekend visits. They just have to realize that Daddy has a roommate, and Daddy's roommate needs a little respect.

Buddy: We're working on that. The youngest looked at Ron one time and said, "Well, this is Papa's apartment."

Ron: I said, "No, this is *ours*. This is *our* apartment. These are *our* things."

****

Ron: My family's very accepting.

Buddy: I love his mom dearly. It's like when we went there a month ago, we walked in, she gives Ron a great big hug, and she lets go of him and comes and gives me the same great big hug. It is wonderful, because I don't have that for Ron with my mom. I take the boys down every other Sunday, so that they see their grandmother. I've wanted Ron to go with me, but he won't go, and I can understand that, because he doesn't want to be introduced as my roommate. I've come a long way, but I still can't tell my mom. On the phone, sometimes, she goes, "I want to come up."

Ron: And I will not take any of the pictures down. There's a picture in the bathroom of a gentleman laying on the couch naked, and we've got other pictures, but I won't take them down if she comes over.

Buddy: And I can deal with that.

Ron: This is my domain--our domain--and I'm not changing it for anyone.

Buddy: She's mentioned she wants to come see my apartment, because she's worried about her little boy, who's going through a divorce and all this.

Ron: She knows I'm here. She knows I do the cleaning and the cooking, because Buddy doesn't like to do it.

Buddy: I know she knows, but I can't come out and tell her. Growing up, there was really no show of affection in our family. I look at it now, after going through my mind, saying, "Why am I gay?" and I truly don't believe that it's environmental, even though I didn't see the family structure the way the books say it should be.

About eighth grade, I realized that there was something different about me, but I didn't want to say that I was....well, we didn't use the word 'gay' back then, and I didn't want to admit that I was, as they called us, 'queer.' I was always an artsy person--into music, dressed different. I'm from Downeast Maine, where you grow up, and of course, you got married before you're eighteen, or you're gay. This was the mentality.

There was this guy that I met in high school, whose name was Terry. We worked at the same job together in the sardine canning factories. We became real good friends, and one thing led to another. We became a couple, but I still denied the fact that I was gay because of the environment that we had to live in.

After high school, I went on to college. Terry went away, but we still saw each other. In college I met the woman who was to become my wife. I knew that I wanted a family, and it was "the thing to do." She graduated the year after I did, and we got married. Terry had been my lover for four or five years, and he was our best man. My wife knew about our relationship, and I'm sure, as many typical women, she thought, "Well, I can change him." And she did for six years.

We were married for six years or better, and I had no thoughts of gay relationships, until one night I got home and walked into the house, and there's Terry and my wife sitting at the dining room table. Well, every emotion known to mankind had to run through my body. I wanted to punch him; I wanted to hug him, anything. We had no contact for over five years. We just sat there and talked, and my wife said she was going to go to bed, so Terry and I decided to go out to the bar and have a couple drinks. We talked, and all those feelings started coming back again, and I tried to deny them. My wife and I had two sons at the time, and that was really important in my life.

I was going through all that turmoil in my mind. My two sons are my life, and I thought, "I can't do this to them." I wasn't really promiscuous, but I would find meetings to go to and would make up meetings to be away. A guy that I was seeing, he and his wife and my wife and I were best friends, so he and I were basically a couple. That lasted almost three years; then he "came out," and he and his wife broke up. I thought, "Oh, my God, guilt by association." Finally, things just started breaking down between my wife and I. It wasn't angry fighting; it wasn't malicious and miserable, but it was just gone.

The hardest thing in my life that I have ever had to do was to sit the boys down and tell them that I was going to leave and that they had nothing to do with it, that it was an adult decision. But the boys and I have become much closer. I have not told them that I am gay. I don't think they're old enough to handle that.

My older son just turned thirteen, so he's going through the adolescent changes and probably questioning his own sexuality. I think that's enough. My younger son just turned eleven in April, and they're totally different personalities. He's happy-go-lucky. He's the type that if I told him, he could deal with it. We sit down and we talk about gay people. When the whole thing on the gays in the military came out, he and I were sitting watching CNN one night. He goes, "Papa, this is so stupid. Gay people have just as much right for a job anywhere they want it as anybody else." I went, "Wow."

But my older son is into the peer group right now. I've got to wait with him. I don't know what their mother has told them, but we have them every other weekend. They come stay here, and they see Ron and I sleeping together, and they accept it, which is good.

(Ron died December 12, 1995)

To Have Known

If I had known the troubles you bore.
If I had only seen the sadness your face silently revealed.
If I had known what gentleness, care
And gladness could have brought...
I would have given more...
More warmth.

What thoughts despair you
I may only think and wonder.
Would my friendship
Have meant more?
I should have slipped my hand within yours
And made you stay.

If I had only known.

-- Gordon Barker

PART 4

Barb
Scott
Catherine
Skip and Walt
Natalie
Bob
Sharon
Ken
Jen and Elizabeth

Barb

I think I get better with every year. I remember being very depressed when I hit 30 and thinking, "I'm not happy where I'm at; I don't want to be here." At 38, I made the choice, and I changed. Ever since then, I have been refining my vision of who I am. It changes gradually, but it doesn't feel like I'm presenting myself with opposites. Things are beginning to feel concurrent.

I remember thinking as a child that when I grow up, I will be grown up. That would be it--stop. It's been interesting to watch and to experience the progress and the maturity in my relationships as a part of going through this. I basically married someone that I cared a lot about, that I loved as a friend, as I understood friendship, and married because I wanted to satisfy my parents' desire for me to be married, but I wanted to do it in a kind of underhanded way by marrying somebody they didn't like and living a life that they would not have chosen for me.

I did my undergraduate work in religion, which, in essence, prepared me for not much of anything, and went on to do graduate work in special education. Once I completed my graduate work, I helped to set up a child care center, which was the first fully integrated child care program in North Carolina. I had married at the beginning of my senior year in college and had two children. They, too, were very much involved in the center and were one of the reasons I kept on keeping on in that program.

I also became involved in the women's movement and in one of the first women's consciousness-raising groups in North

Carolina. I was barefoot and pregnant and wondering what on earth I was doing. A number of the women in the group were lesbians. We supported the women on campus who were striking for union recognition, higher wages, and quality child care at a reasonable cost, and then helped to create this center. We also created a children's press, which is still in existence, and wrote alternative children's books. It was a very interesting period of time in my life.

I had a woman friend I'd admired from a distance for a number of years, who had come out very early in the beginning of our consciousness-raising group. I listened to her struggles in seeking counseling and support and realized that there were very few people out in that world who were going to support anybody who made that kind of choice. Several years later, she made the choice to commit suicide. That just knocked me over. I knew that I couldn't sit on the fence any longer. For whatever reason, her taking her life was not something that I wanted to let go unspoken. Without my ever saying it to her, and regretting that I'd never taken the opportunity to say it to her, she'd had a tremendous influence on me in a positive way. I felt it was time to do something about it.

I was incredibly unhappy. My gut said that I couldn't live that way and be honorable to my then-partner, my children, and more importantly, to me. I was doing the very traditional female thing by trying to be all things to all people, and what I really needed to do was to look at me. Once I was able to say to myself-- not even to anyone else--"Yes, you are a lesbian," and use the 'L' word and see myself as someone who was woman-identified and very comfortable with that, it was like a piece of a puzzle that had been missing had been put in place for me.

I made the decision and within a week had said, "I'm leaving," and had plans for it to go relatively slowly. We lived in a large enough house that my expectation was that we could live in separate quarters, share responsibilities for the children, and do something very gradual. That was not to be. He was too angry, and it was really not safe for me to stay, so I left. We shared custody of the children for a period of time, and then he became very angry and started stalking me. At that point, I said I really need to take this seriously and leave the state. I had every intention that my children would go with me, but they made the choice, including my daughter, that they wanted to stay with him. Being angry with me entered into that. I think one of the hardest things I ever did in my life was know that I needed to go and leave them behind.

I didn't have anyone else supporting me in the decision to leave. Everyone felt very strongly that I should stay, regardless of cost. I didn't choose to leave right away. I stayed for six to eight months before I moved, but it was incredibly painful to walk into a grocery store and have people that I'd known for years turn around and walk the other way. I thought, "I'm really the same person in most ways. I'm only a more honest person at this point."

I think had anyone told me the changes that that decision I was making were going to bring to my life and also to my children's lives, it wouldn't have changed what I did, but it might have changed how I went about it; I did not feel at the time that I had a choice. I had been living a lie for a lot of years, and I was to the point of seeing suicide as a creative alternative and knew that that was not where I wanted to be.

I'd grown used to a relatively comfortable lifestyle. I'd grown used to the security of knowing that there would always be a double income. I upended all of that for me and for the kids and knew that in declaring my sexuality, that I also put myself at risk for being able to ever fight a custody battle for my children. The lawyers knew that I had no chance in hell to win a custody fight for those kids. I also knew, as a child care director and a person in the field for fourteen years, that I'd only seen one separation and divorce involving children that had been handled in a loving way. I knew that regardless of what I wanted for the children, if I didn't honor what they wanted, that I was sunk and so were they and that I would need to look at different ways of having a relationship with them, if I was the non-custodial, long-distance parent.

Ultimately, that's been a wonderful gift, because it's allowed me to be relatively objective with my children, a person that they seek for advice. I truly believe that they have a right to make choices for themselves. I honor them and will support them as best I can. I'll let them know when I disagree, but that doesn't change, or shouldn't change, what they choose to do. That's a unique relationship and one that I really enjoy having with both of them, but it's been a long time in coming. It's allowed us, when we are together, to spend real quality time. We don't *do* a lot; we try to *be* a lot with one another, because our time is very limited.

I don't know that there's anything that I can say I wish never happened. Every one of those years was a year I grew in some way around some thing. I had to get through all those stages and ages.

One of the greatest challenges for me has been my relationship with Jean and the differences in our realities. If anybody had told me that I would be in a wonderfully intimate and loving relationship with a chartered financial consultant who is a

Republican and conservative, I would have said, "You're crazy. Never, ever, ever would I do that." We knew each other, and we both had stereotyped images of each other. She saw me as the radical hippie, "out" dyke, and I saw her as the so-she-thinks-she's-so-closeted, short, cute, professional dyke. I mean, anybody could look at her and know she was a dyke.

She'd been told by a very close friend of hers that I was someone worth knowing, and we just acknowledged each other from a distance. I would see her regularly at the Y, and she eventually asked me out for lunch. We had a good time talking and pursued our friendship from there. We both, at the time, were in the process of ending the relationships we were in and knew that we did not want to muddy the waters for either our friendship or those relationships. So, we worked on maintaining a friendship and said that if we got to a point where it is comfortable for us to pursue something more, we know that the desire is probably there. We got to that point and decided yes, we were real serious about looking at this. It was a very nice progression.

My two previous relationships were ones that had started very quickly and moved into a relationship without really exploring a friendship. This time I was feeling more centered about who I was, and I certainly had had an opportunity to know what some unhealthy relationships could be, both with a man and with women. I wanted to make sure that my needs were being met, but I had to figure out what those were, knowing that my attraction and my love for her as a friend were all mixed in there. It has made for a very warm, loving, and healthy relationship, with its moments of struggle and disagreement. I don't have any expectation that she's going to be any different than she is. I love her for all of those parts of who she is. She doesn't have any

171

expectation that I'm going to be much different, either. I think the part that we're enjoying is getting to know more fully who each other is.

For me, it's the first time I've shared a relationship with someone whom I respect from a professional point of view, as well as from a lover and partner point of view. We talk about our work, and we critique each other's work, which is unique. I love my work. I direct the programs in most of two counties for children at risk. It's a very exciting job.

I'm not sure I understand what I'm in the midst of, but I'm hoping I understand better where I came from and hope to God that I have a vision of where I'm going. But then there are days, when I wouldn't admit it to very many people, but all I want to do is to be able to sit with an iced tea in my hand and play the social game and not have to worry about being competent or making money or being responsible, where I want to give up this 'be-responsible' role and just be cared for. I know that there are days that Jean feels the same way. Fortunately, we can trade off those days and just say, "It's okay, feel that way."

****

There are lots of different kinds of human beings within any one category, and categories are artificially applied. I just had a discussion yesterday with three other women. All of us identify ourselves as lesbians, yet we were trying to discuss the whole issue of bisexuality and where we stood, individually. Where do I stand as a woman who has experienced heterosexual sex and yet did not then and do not now identify myself as heterosexual? Where do other women stand, who have enjoyed heterosexual sex, but realize that that is not their primary way of wanting to relate sensually or emotionally to an adult and have made the choice to make their primary relationships with a woman? There are all different kinds of combinations and permutations, and I realized that all of us need to feel the freedom of making those kinds of discreet choices for our personal selves.

My daughter has talked with me. She came to me when she was thirteen and said, "Mom, I want to be sexually active." My jaw dropped, and I said, "Well, I have prepared you for this, although I'm not sure I want this," but she made a conscious choice to become sexually active. I forewarned her, forearmed her, and got her all set up with a friend of mine who was a public health nurse, and she went from there. Afterwards, she came to me and said, "Is this all there is?" I said, "Well, there's a lot more to intimate relationships than just 'doing it.'" She talked about, "I think maybe I want to step back and look at this in a different light."

She's always been very cautious in her relationships, but over the last several years, she has not been involved with men. She had a high school friend of hers that she was visiting acknowledge to her that she was a lesbian and that she was attracted to her. My daughter said, "You know, Mom, that didn't feel uncomfortable at all. It felt exciting. It felt like something I might want to consider exploring." I said, "I will support you in whatever you decide you want to do for you, but know that it's for you, and know that any choice you make now can be changed and that there are lots of different options. Also know that when you become involved in a lesbian lifestyle that there are prices to be paid and that you do need to take on a different level of cautiousness in your life. Probably one of the wisest women to talk to is Jean."

She spent some time talking to Jean, because she knew Jean had been married, too. Jean said, "If you're attracted to both, if you enjoy being with men and you enjoy being with women, give yourself a break and take the easier road. For me, I had to realize that as much as I loved the man that I was with, my primary attraction and my primary spiritual energy went to women. I didn't have a choice in that respect." That is true for me, as well. I don't have a choice. It's not a preference. It is an orientation. It is something I have; it is me.

Jean told her, "If you have that choice, then look at your options, because you know that there's going to be pain involved if you choose to be a lesbian." It was real important for Jean to be the one to have said that to her. I just want her to be happy. Lord knows, I spent too many years trying to fit a mold that didn't fit, and I want both my children to feel comfortable with who they are. The greatest gift I can give them is being who I am and showing the struggles involved in making that choice.

Scott

I didn't want to date when I was in high school, but my parents kept pushing me, "How come you don't date? How come you don't go to the prom?" Then I remember all of a sudden waking up one day and thinking, "My God, I'm gay. I like men." Somehow making that connection of how I felt and putting the word with it, having an identity, made things much easier to understand. Overnight, all the confusion was gone. I knew that I was attracted to men. I knew that I didn't have an attraction to women. Girls were my best friends, and the friendships that I had with them went way beyond a dating level; but I didn't want to date girls.

As a kid trying to come to terms with your homosexuality, it makes you really doubt yourself. It makes you wonder if you're different or if you're crazy. Today, I accept my sexuality. It's a hard thing to accept. I didn't choose it or go out and say, "Gee, I think I'll be gay today, because I love to be discriminated against." I don't go running down the halls at school saying, "Guess what! I'm gay, and I have AIDS"; but I'm comfortable.

My parents never talked to me about sex, either. Who's going to go to their parents when they're in high school and say, "I've got these feelings. Can we talk about sex? I like men." I don't blame my parents for my being HIV-positive, but I have to honestly say that I think that a lack of education is why the HIV is with me now. I became infected as a senior in college, so it's been three years.

I'd never heard a talk about safer sex. I didn't know what a condom was. When I was in college, a condom was something you put around the faucet in the bathroom, filled with water, and dropped out the dormitory window. It wasn't something you used for safer sex.

When I came out to my parents, we had this huge blow-up. My entire world was shattered. I thought, "There must be something wrong with me. I can't be gay; I've got to change. I've got to do something about this." In the matter of an hour, everything that had been was gone. I was still who I was and they were still who they were, but for two years after that blow-up, the relationship was very strained.

I was a junior at the University when I told my mom. I got this real strange look of disbelief from her, and then I got this outrage. She wasn't going to carry this knowledge alone. I *had* to tell my father, and it was *me* who was going to tell him. So we told my dad when he got home. Then I got hit with everything from: "God didn't make you this way; if He had, everybody would be this way; I'll never have grandchildren now, because you're gay; well, you're involved in the arts, and people are like that sometimes in the arts"; to: "You're just really confused and trying to be accepted." It was the worst night of my life. It was worse than telling my parents I was HIV-positive, because deep-down, I knew that when I told them I was positive, there would be love there. When I told my parents I was gay, it was pure hatred and lashing out. It was blame anybody in the world that you can blame.

For months after, my parents didn't want to speak to me. I called every week to make sure they knew I was okay. I spent Christmas at their house and it was very quiet, but the next day,

176

my dad lost it, and all my mom could say was, "Do you see what you've done to your father?"

They canceled my car insurance. I was on their policy, but they decided that they could no longer afford it, so I was taken off. I drove my car to their yard and parked it. It sat there for a year, and I took the bus to student teach. They went to counseling and slowly began to realize that it wasn't my fault; but it is a subject that was never talked about again.

Last summer, the day after my former partner died, I called to tell them he had died and lost it on the phone. It had been two years since our blow-up, and things were still a bit strained. He died of spinal meningitis, so I wasn't lying when I told them that; but my mom said to me, "You can hang up. You can get as pissed off as you want, but I want to know, 'Did he die of AIDS?'" Before my mind could work, I said, "Yes." My mom started to say "I expect you to go get yourself tested," but again, my mind was either racing so fast that I didn't realize what was going on, or it had shut down completely. I said, "I have been, Mom, and I'm positive." Suddenly, it was out. It wasn't intentional, but it was out. My mom lost it. Finally I said, "When you calm down, call me back," and I hung up the phone. They called back and within a half hour came down to visit. It was the only time I've ever seen my dad choke back emotion. It was all self-blame, "My God, we've done this to you. What could we have done to prevent this?"

Now, my parents don't ask a lot of questions about the gay thing. They do ask a lot about the AIDS issue. They're concerned about that and very supportive. I can't imagine having more love and support than I do from them now.

177

The gay issue doesn't matter at this point. That shows how petty a problem it really is. It isn't an issue. The HIV thing really turned them around and, you know, if it came down to choosing between having the disease and having all the love and support that I have now, or not having the disease and having my old relationship with my parents, I would choose the disease, because there's more love there than I could imagine.

I've never had a heterosexual relationship, so I have nothing to compare it to, but I know what it feels like to be in a homosexual relationship. I know I like the strength that I find in another man's arms.

Would I change? Given the way the world is today, yes, I would. If the world were more tolerant, if the world were more accepting, then I'd say no, because I am perfectly happy with the way I am. But because of the way the world is, I'm sad to say, yes, I would change and wish to be what society calls "normal." I'm proud of who I am, but I'm not a fool. So if somebody said to me, "You have a choice to make today. I can make you straight, and you can live the rest of your life as a heterosexual man, or you can stay gay," I'd take the deal. Even if it meant I'd lose Peter, I'd still have to take it, because I am so tired of being discriminated against.

Whenever I've dated, it's always been, "I'll meet you at five, and we'll go to some little restaurant in a city 150 miles away, where there isn't anybody that we're going to chance running into." We'll sit across the table from each other, in a restaurant with candles, but we can't look in the other person's eyes, because someone might know that we're gay.

There are certain things you can't say, because it sounds "queer." You can't hold hands in a movie theater. It's pitch

178

black, but you still can't hold hands. As a romantic, I can go and watch "Dr. Zhivago" and cry my eyes out, but I can't cry my eyes out with somebody who's male, because that would mean I'm gay.

Imagine yourself dating. It doesn't matter if it's a male or a female. For a week you see that person as often as you can, but nobody can see you together, so you can't go anywhere in public. Try to hide that relationship for a week and you'll see how difficult it is.

I can go to the park on the fourth of July and see couples sitting together, holding hands and listening to music; but I can't have that. I have to hide that affection. I can't express the warmth and love that other people are entitled to show, because I love someone of the same sex. It's hard to stifle down all those feelings. Then, when you're alone with this person you love, there's so much to express, you don't know where to start; or it's so smothered that you can't even begin.

I don't think most people know what a homosexual lifestyle is. They don't realize that you go to bed at night, you get up in the morning, you brush your teeth, you wash, you go to work or go to school, you come home, you eat, you change, you feel. It's just that the central person that you feel for or have emotions for happens to be of the same sex. It's difficult for me to understand why someone has a hard time with that, because to me, it's normal. I haven't known anything else.

(Scott died November 16, 1995, at 26 years of age.)

Catherine

Growing up, there was something that looked after me and that taught me, that put people in my path so that I could get needs met that I wasn't getting met through my family. I believe that I was being pulled along by some other force. I'm sure that we all are.

My first experience with death was when my friend Paul died. He was seventeen when he got hit by a car. After his death, I was standing outside with his five-year-old cousin, who didn't understand where Paul was and why he wasn't coming back. It was a clear night sky with a lot of stars. I said, "Well, you know, any time you want to talk to Paul, all you've got to do is talk to him." She looked up and said, "See that star right there? That's Paul." I said, "OK, let's talk to him." So she starts talking: "Paul, why won't you come home? I want you to be here with me. We miss you. It's time to come home, Paul." I was standing behind her, bawling, and thinking it's so sad that this five-year-old doesn't understand death. Paul wouldn't listen to her, so she said, "Well, see that star over there? That's Jesus," and she started talking to Jesus, saying that she wanted Paul back now and asking Jesus to send Paul home. She finally decided, "Well, if you're not going to send Paul home, I want you to take care of him until I can come see him."

Ever since then, when I need to talk to Paul, I go outside at night. I find the brightest star in the sky, the star that she pointed to for Paul, and his presence is always there.

When my uncle died five years ago, that star came to represent him for me, because he was the most recent loss in my life. Then when my sister, Sarah, died, the star represented her. I think about her every day, and at night I go outside, I look up, and there she is. It's not a sad thing for me. It's a peaceful thing.

I think about what that five-year-old did for me. She innocently made sense of something that we, as adults, complicate. We all need something that's tangible, something we can see, something we can count on being there after someone dies to help us deal with their death, whether it's a picture we can put up in a room, a grave site that we can visit, or a star.

It's been an interesting journey. When I look at the things that I've been through, I have this feeling that something has put me on a path, taught me to be who I am, and pulled me through, because literally, there are times in my life when I should have been dead. I've been suicidal many times, and the fact that I'm here today is a miracle. There has to be a reason.

My parents got divorced when I was three. I don't remember much of it, because I was so young. I didn't find out until I was nineteen years old that my mother has a mental illness. That's why my father divorced her. He was married to her for seven years and now tells vivid stories about how she tried to kill him. He tells me those things, so that I'll understand why he divorced her.

My mother got custody of all three children. I don't know how, but the judge gave her custody, and we moved to Florida. My father never called, and he never wrote. We went through years of mental and physical torment, and no one told us that she was mentally ill. I ran away from home when I was fourteen. The police kept making me go home, until finally, I ran away so many times, they decided to let me be. I loved my mother, but I was very angry with her for the way she treated me. In spite of that, though, I have an immense amount of respect for a woman who can try to raise three children while going through what she was going through in her own mind and what she goes through now.

I have no respect for my father. He's a man who has no physical impairments. He has a beautiful house, lots of land, two beautiful cars, and has lived that way his entire life. I grew up wearing Goodwill clothes, hand-me-downs from my brother, not always knowing where we were going to get our next meal.

I dropped out of the ninth grade to work, because bills weren't getting paid, and we needed the money. I got my G.E.D. when I was eighteen, but I didn't think that college was ever possible. A friend of mine convinced me that I was smart enough and I could do it. So here I am. I graduate on May 8th. This is a big thing for me.

I never dated when I was younger. I never went out. I didn't care about guys. I never really thought about girls, either. I just decided that I didn't have a sexuality. It wasn't something that was important to me. Then I decided people were going to start thinking I'm weird, so I better start dating. I had a horrible first experience, and that was the end of my dating career.

I decided that perhaps I was meant to be a nun, that I wasn't meant to have sexuality. I knew I didn't want to be a nun, but that would be the only way society would accept me for not having sex. A normal, everyday human being, who was a virgin, they wouldn't accept.

Eventually, I came here and met a woman. I knew that she was a lesbian, and I, being the worldly person that I was, decided to tell her that it was okay with me, as long as she understood that I wasn't a lesbian. It's unbelievable to me how clueless I was.

I used to sing to her, and I'd know that I'd be feeling things, but I was in denial about this. After a while of having this chemistry, I realized I had these feelings. I cried and cried. I couldn't believe it. I was so confused, but then I became comfortable with my sexuality.

I was involved with this woman for about three years. We were not compatible enough to have a long-term relationship, but we are still the best of friends. In the next few years, I'd really like to work on a relationship with someone. I want to have someone to share my life with. I want to settle down. I'd like to buy a house. I'd like to have a career.

Sometimes it's scary, though, to think of the things that can happen and that have happened to people in the past for being "out." So I don't walk around with a big button on my shirt, and I'm not out to people who I don't feel it's relevant to be out to; but I'm out to my family. In the last two years, I've made it a point to come out to them all, because I didn't want to be worried about whether or not they'd love me if they really knew me. I've lost relationships with some of my relatives who will just not have anything to do with me. They loved me to death before, but now they can't have anything to do with me. That's an issue for them to deal with, not an issue for me. I value who I am, and I know I'm a good person.

Skip and Walt

Skip: We've been together close to thirty years now, and we've always worked together, never against each other.

Walt: All through the years we've been together, I'll bet we haven't had a fight. Occasionally, we have an argument, but otherwise, we compromise. Sometimes I'll be thinking about something, and he'll bring it up, and I'll say, "I was just thinking about that." That's how close our thoughts have developed over the years.

Skip: We've been together since 1965. If it hadn't been for him, I probably would have been dead years ago, the way I was going. I was drunk every night, fighting, and doing all sorts of crazy shit.

At the time, I was going to the University, and I was working at an ice cream parlor part-time to pay for my car. I was drunker than a skunk one night. That's how I met Walt. I was so drunk I couldn't walk, so he picked me up. You can guess the rest. For a long time, I hated him. I really did, and I thought I'd dumped him. Then all of a sudden one night, he showed up out where I worked, and I almost died, because here I am supposed to be real straight and drinking with all these tough friends. Here he shows up, sitting at the counter, and oh, my Jesus, what am I going to do now? I kept trying to avoid him, and he kept coming back.

Walt: It was basically love at first sight, when I first saw Skip. He couldn't get rid of me.

185

Skip: I fought with myself for a long time. Then reality set in.

Walt: I think he actually felt that I cared for him. I tried to keep his liquor down. By then, I had stopped drinking, so I didn't drink hardly at all, and we done things together. He admitted that I was good for him.

Skip: We was off and on again for about three years, and then I finally just accepted it and said, "that's the way I am, and I'm not going to change. Piss on it." I had a steady girlfriend, and I was thinking about getting married. I knew deep down I didn't want to, but I knew what my parents were expecting. I think that was half of my drinking problem right there. Finally, I just said, "The hell with it, that's what I'm going to be, and if people don't like it, go to hell." And we've been together ever since.

My mother never knew about Walt and me. I think she might have surmised it, but if she did, she never said nothing.

Walt: I knew I was gay all my life, ever since I was young. I acknowledged it to myself, no one else. Just like today, I don't tell no one. It's none of their business. I'll be at work, and they probably know I am, but they don't say nothing, because I act normal. I don't bother them; they don't bother me. I'm out on the road all the time anyhow, so basically, I'm alone. I don't deny it, but I don't publicize it.

I know my younger brother is gay. I have an uncle that I know was gay. It runs in the family, I think. It's in your genes. I think it starts out your thoughts are that way when you're born. I don't know, I just feel comfortable with a male, that's all.

Skip: I think a lot of gay relationships don't last, because I don't think a lot of people really want them to last. There are a few that do get along and do make it. We work hard at it seven days a week, and that ain't always fun.

Walt: It's compromise all the time. To hell with arguments. I don't want to argue. It ain't worth it. If you're going to live together, you got to get along. Why fight? Life is too short. As years progress, we get to think like each other. Now, we just about know each other's thoughts.

Natalie

I've been with my partner, now, for sixteen years. It'll be seventeen years in August. We're good friends.

I became aware of my sexual orientation being different in college. In high school I dated, went to all the dances, the proms, and all those things. There were six of us that palled around together a lot. We were all Catholic. I would say that I had a real strong interest in two of my female friends. Never acted on it and didn't understand it, but in college I acted on it, and that was, "Oh wow, great!"

I was in my mid-twenties and had been in this lesbian relationship for quite a few years, and I was dating this lawyer, Ted. We used to do a lot of dancing, a lot of skiing, and we had a lot of fun together. We were very committed to each other, and he asked me to marry him. We planned it all out. He was Greek Orthodox, so we had it down to the details of the different clergy and different music. I had my gown, and my bridesmaids had their gowns, and for February break from school, we drove down to Florida because he had never met my parents. We were there for a week.

During that week, I started my period, and I had wicked bad cramps, so I went into my mother's room to sleep, but I couldn't sleep. She had Jeanne Dixon's book, *The Gift of Prophecy*, on the side of her bed, so I started reading it. What amazed me is I never knew my mother to be a reader, so I was surprised even to see the book there--and then the contents! It was, I think, the first book I had ever read about psychic phenomena and predictions. It really bothered me, because I had been told all along, if you're Catholic, you don't believe in this stuff.

I had been so confused with my own personal experiences of seeing Spirit and searching in different religions all through college. Then I come home, and my mother has this book, and I thought, "I'll be damned." I asked her, "What's going on? You're telling me if you're Catholic, these are sins, and it's the work of the devil. What are you talking about?" "Oh, Natalie, it's only a book." I said, "Yeah, only a book."

All these years, I'd been trying to talk to her about exactly the same thing. It was, "No, no, no," and then, "Here it is. You're reading about it; you're talking about it; you're approving it, because someone famous did it." It blew me away, and I began my search, finding that there was more to life than what I'd read about before.

I didn't discuss it with Ted, but as we got into the car to drive back to Massachusetts, I said, "Ted, have you ever heard of the book, *Gift of Prophecy* by Jeanne Dixon?" He kind of mumbled, and he knew I was very excited. Then he turned and just glared at me, and he said, "I never want to hear you talk about that ever again, and I suppose you believe in the evil eye, too." I didn't know what the evil eye was, but that was interesting, and I wanted to know more about it, but that was that. We drove all the way back in silence. As far as I was concerned, if I couldn't think for myself, there was a serious problem here. We got back home, and he wanted to come in and talk. I said, "I really don't see any reason to talk now. We had 33 hours in which to talk." So I gave his ring back, and I called home and told them it was off. That was the end of that.

****

I've always enjoyed athletics immensely. When I was in college in my junior year, we won the Women's State Volleyball Championship, and we were preparing for the Southeastern Volleyball Championships. We were practicing at the elementary school gym. I was a spiker. My set-up went a little high and above me. I went for it. I hit it and I landed in the bleachers. I hurt my back wicked bad, but I went back and played, then got back to the dorm and went to take a shower. I couldn't move. I was in excruciating pain. They called my parents, took me to the hospital, and wanted to do surgery, but my parents said, "Absolutely no!" and flew me home. I forget how many months I was in the hospital, but I was there awhile. I was paralyzed from the waist down.

Finally, they were going to do surgery this one morning, and I had a 50-50 chance of regaining any movement in my lower body. I think I was nineteen, and I was petrified because playing sports was my life. Now I was facing the fact that I may never walk again. This particular morning that they were going to do the surgery, I woke up very early, just at sunrise, and I had my first *real* realization of an inner connection with something. I saw this glow of light at the foot of my bed that then began to emerge into a larger and larger ball of light. Then that ball of white light took shape and formed what was my understanding of Jesus.

I don't know if anyone else in the room could have heard it, but I was the only one in the room, and I heard Him say-- whether in my mind, mind to mind, or verbal-- "If you follow me, you'll be OK." It was like, "Oh, yes!" I don't mean to make light of it, but I was young; I was petrified; they were telling me I wasn't ever going to walk again; and then, lo and behold, as clear

191

as you're sitting there and I'm sitting here, I see this ball of light emerge, and here's Jesus, and I hear Him say that. As soon as I had made that recognition, that acceptance, that agreement, the light diminished. The form intertwined with rainbow colored lights and white light, and then it was just this ball of light again. It faded into a nickel or a dime and disappeared. I was in awe. I didn't know where I was. Tears were streaming down my eyes, because it was so powerful.

I don't know how long after, but not very long, a nurse came in to give me a shot to take me down for surgery. I said, "No," and I refused any treatment. They didn't know what they were going to do with me. They were going to have to call my parents. "I don't care who you call; I'm not going to have surgery," I said. "I can feel. I know that I can walk," and here I was, still in traction.

Well, the nurse gave up on me and called the doctor, and he tried to reason with me, but there was no reasoning. I didn't explain to them. I just said, "There's nothing I need. I'm fine." So he ran his little tracing wheel up and down my leg and stuck pins in. I said, "Yes, I can feel it," and he said something inane like, "Well, I guess we kept her in traction long enough; things are adjusting."

I've never experienced so much pain in my life as when the feeling started coming back in my legs. It was like, whoa-a-a-a, I said yes to this? But it was only temporary. In no time at all, with the therapy that they did, I went back to college.

The doctor told me things like, "Well, you were very fortunate, but you can never bowl and no horseback riding and no waterskiing." Get serious! Tell me some-thing I can't play, and in my mind it's, "Yeah, yeah, yeah, I'll say anything; just let me out

192

of here." I had heard someone else who is a greater authority than this doctor tell me that if I followed Him, I'd be fine, and I believed it. So I immediately went back and played every sport I could and did very well. I made three all-star teams at Florida State that year: basketball, volleyball, and softball. The first basketball game I played after I got back, I scored 50 points. I'll never forget that one.

I was raised Catholic, and I never got a lot of answers that I needed for my personal awareness. The rest of my junior year and my senior year I went to every church on campus seeking more spiritual awareness, more spiritual knowledge, to have things make sense to me, like why Jesus had come to see me. After that, I also realized that I intuitively knew when a professor was going to give a pop test. I would be shown what pages to study, and I would read those pages. That's the only way I got through college, I swear.

I wanted to know more and really started studying. I had had these experiences and hadn't really paid attention to them. My accident experience was pivotal, but I still didn't recognize it. It was not until I was 28, which was about ten years later, and after having read *The Gift of Prophecy* that it finally sank in. I was searching in every church, every synagogue, but it wasn't until Spiritualism that it all made sense for me.

I had to find out everything I could about Spiritualism, about psychic phenomena. I discovered a whole new shelf in the library on the subjects and found a local church which I started attending. I began my courses of study there and enrolled in the Morris Pratt Institute for ordination and studied there. I felt totally at home with the philosophy, and everything made sense. I'd seen the spirits of people who had passed since I was a little kid. I didn't realize it was other than what everybody else was seeing.

It changed my whole world. There was much, much more peace in my heart. I've dedicated my life now to teaching what I know. Healing has been a part of this, because of that time I had the visitation, but I don't think death is negative. It's just a transition. We see it constantly in nature. It's an experience of life, the next stage. We are here on this earth for a short time. It's what we do in that time that counts.

Bob

When I was growing up, there used to be incredible fights--
I mean, physical abuse and beatings. There would be guns
involved sometimes, where my father would threaten to shoot my
mother, and she'd threaten to shoot him. Once he set the house on
fire. He used to beat my mother in front of us. That was the
worst thing to experience, because he'd be beating her, and we'd
all be beating on him to get him off from her.

He worked on construction, so he had access to dynamite,
and for a long time, he threatened to blow us up. He said he was
going to kill us. Then one night he didn't come home, and he
didn't call. It was two or three o'clock in the morning, and my
mother gets all of us children up, and she says she's heard a noise
down cellar. She says, "Your father's down there; he's going to
blow us up." We're living in fear anyway, so at two o'clock in the
morning, we're up, because we're afraid that our father's going to
blow the house up. We're outside, and I sneak up to the cellar
door and open it, and we're throwing rocks down there, telling
him, "Daddy, Daddy, please don't blow us up. We don't want to
die." Honest to God. Well, he wasn't going to blow us up. He
was working, but he didn't call us to let us know.

He was a good provider, though. He made little money,
but we always ate well; we always had plenty of clothes to wear.
We were always warm; we always had a roof over our head, and
we always went to all the school activities. He would take us to

195

dances at the school, and then he'd be waiting out front, sitting there at twelve o'clock at night.

My mother was very supportive, and she smothered us with love and affection. My three sisters and I have all done very well. None of us are criminals or a detriment to society. I attribute a lot of that to my mother, because she was there giving us the emotional rearing and strength that we needed during those really traumatic periods.

****

I didn't really become sexually aware until I was in the fifth or sixth grade. I was a slow bloomer, but I was aware of being curious about men as far back as I can remember. When I was in kindergarten, I would be curious being in the men's room at the urinals when the older boys would be there. Something always made me aware that I had an attraction towards men. It just took me a number of years to really understand it, because of society's belief and my rearing. My mother was very religious, and to her, homosexuality was wrong. It was the whole Sodom and Gomorrah thing. I remember people in the community where I grew up, who were thought of as being homosexuals, were ridiculed and made fun of, and I didn't want that.

Even though I knew I had an attraction towards men, I wanted a girlfriend, because everybody else had a girlfriend, and that was the "normal" thing to do. I can remember in the fifth grade being friendly with one girl. When they used to have movies, we always made sure that we got over in the corner, and instead of sitting there watching the movie, we'd write little silly love notes back and forth.

I became very aware of my homosexuality in high school, though, once I had gone through puberty and my hormones were going crazy. I tried heterosexual sex and was not satisfied. I didn't have that much homosexual contact in high school, but there were a few instances where guys would masturbate together--that type of thing. I was extremely turned on by it, and I used to fantasize about it, so I knew, then, this was me. Fortunately, at that time in your life, young men do experiment with masturbation with other individuals, so even though you did it, it didn't mean you were a faggot or a queer, and I didn't pursue it.

Being gay makes you feel so negative. You feel so dirty. The whole religious beliefs about God and Sodom and Gomorrah and it's not natural. I have to spend a lot of time telling myself that I am not worthless, that I am a very successful person, that I've accomplished a lot in my life. I'm not a brain surgeon, but I'm an intelligent man and I have value; I have something to offer society; there's a good being inside me. I have to work at that all the time. Everybody says, "We don't care if you're gay, but just don't talk about it. Just keep it in the closet."

Racism, too, is so rampant in our society. I have found that a lot of heterosexual black men, who I've gotten to know and who have found out that I'm gay, are more accepting of me than straight white men. We're sharing a minority, and they know what that pain is, because they know what it's like to be persecuted. There is a bonding there. They don't want to be physical, and I don't want to be either, but it's incredible that once they know that I am, we can openly talk about it. They can understand where I'm coming from, because of what they've been through, where most heterosexual white men are very bigoted, and the homophobia thing just takes over. They get so nerved up, they can't even talk.

My father and I don't talk about homosexuality. When I first told him that I was gay, he told me to get out of his (blank) house, so I left. Now, it's such a traumatic thing to go near him, because the whole thing starts all over. My stomach churns and tightens up into a big ball. It's like living on eggshells, so I'm better off staying away from him.

But I'm very fortunate, because two of my sisters have accepted my homosexuality completely. Even my brother-in-laws and I talk openly about homosexuality. They know that I'm not one of the thong, dog collar types. They know that I fit into the mainstream of the gay community, which is the majority, and the mainstream of society. So I've got a very good support group there.

Sharon

About eight years ago, I got into recovery for alcoholism and drug addiction, after years of drinking and using other drugs, as well as a history of sexual abuse. All the perpetrators were men and boys.

I've gone the whole gamut in religions, from being raised moderate to real conservative, constricting, and condemning religions. Now I'm in a very liberal community, but the conservative religion part creeps in and creates conflicts for me. If I was to act on what I wanted to, there's still that naggy sort of thing: "What if those people were right? What if I am going to hell? What if there is a hell?" I definitely know in my head that you have to be nuts to buy all of that, hook, line, and sinker, yet it's so insidious. It still creeps back into this liberal mind of mine.

I'm still in the beginning stages of exploring my sexuality. I think I fell in love with a woman this year, but I never told her for fear of losing our friendship. I talk with a liberal spiritual advisor, especially around admitting to myself that I fell in love with a woman. It was real important for me to have somebody with a spiritual grounding who could help me with the fear and other feelings like that.

My therapist wanted me to write some kind of love story that involved a man. I couldn't do it. I couldn't think that way. It was almost like I was becoming obsessed with the woman I fell in love with. Really frustrating and sad, lonely, but that experience opened me up to more of myself and also to begin to question my sexuality.

I think politically, I would feel comfortable if I was to identify myself strictly as lesbian, though it's far safer to align myself as a heterosexual. Probably the nearest thing to reality is that I'm bisexual, but I haven't wanted to take that on, because of the isolation and the criticisms from both camps. I've had a couple of roommates who've lived here at different times, who were lesbian, and they both had real negative things to say about people who are bisexual; and this was long before I was even putting words to it for myself.

It still keeps me a little lost. I'm open to new things, but I still have a fear of relationships with men. I also think that the quality of my friendships with women is so much deeper and more respectful than with men. I have some male friends who are very nice men, who are very sensitive and kind, but I couldn't imagine myself in a relationship with them. I guess lately, I feel more attracted to women.

Ken

I think the old statement "the truth will set you free" is very true. I've felt that it's wrong if I can't be honest and aboveboard with people and do what I think is right. My parents always said to me, "If you can look in the mirror at the end of the day and face yourself and feel like you've done the best job you can do, that's the most important thing."

I grew up, fortunately, in a family where there was never any prejudice expressed under any circumstances about anyone. We never heard derogatory terms. That influenced me in my own self-respect, to know that "queer" or "fairy" or words like that would never be used.

I've never felt anything but that I was gay. I've always known that. I remember being different, but I didn't know what it was until I was in eighth grade or a freshman. My sister or somebody gave me a book on homosexuality and said, "Here it is; read it and understand it." Then they gave me a book on reproduction and said, "Here, this is how it's all done." It was very graphically illustrated. It was very openly talked about when I was in seventh, eighth grade and a freshman.

There's never been a question in my family about me being gay, and I feel very close to them. My parents knew since I was in puberty, and I talked to them about it. The only request I made of them was, "I will talk to you about anything. I'll talk to anybody about anything, but if you have any questions, ask me.

I'm the one who is gay, not anybody else. If you want to know what it's like to be gay, ask me."

When people say this is a preference, it isn't a preference. It really is an orientation, and it does have its drawbacks. I think the loneliness at times becomes very difficult--the feeling of alienation from people. I'm very fortunate that I have a lot of friends. I don't judge friends on sexuality. I have gay friends; I have straight friends. Some of my friends who are straight have never talked to me about being gay. They know. I think when the right moment comes, we'll talk about it.

Basically, I feel very comfortable about my sexuality. I also think that all peoples' lives are very similar. I mean, I put my pants on one leg at a time, and I have the same emotions and the same feelings.

There's not a gay subculture. We're much more diverse than that as people. We are unique individuals, just as everyone is a unique individual. I also think that gay people really seek that monogamous, long-term relationship sort of thing. Although it's supposedly a straight concept, I think that everybody wants it. It's just normal for people to want that.

Speaking about relationships, I tend to find that I'm hit upon as much or equally by married men as I am by gay men. I think some of the men who are hitting on me are probably straight but are out looking for a little gratification. I don't care if a person is gay and married or straight and married, it's absolutely off-limits. Anybody who's in a relationship is totally off-limits. There's not even a question.

I think being "out" has the ability to help other people who are in the closet. Being in the closet is really a torment. There's a large percentage of alcoholism, drug abuse, and self-hate in the

202

gay population, and it's really important for people to see that you can live a happy, contented life and still be gay. You can be respected and be where you want to be in your life. I think one of the reasons a lot of us want to lead publicly open lives is in order to show other people that you can live a whole life.

Jen and Elizabeth

Elizabeth: Our first year together, there were struggles. My mother died, and then my father was sick.

Jen: When Elizabeth moved in, her father came with her.

Elizabeth: He was diabetic. When he moved in, he had both legs, but his legs were bothering him, and he couldn't live alone.

Jen: So, they moved in together. It was a really rough first year. I thought, when she moved in, everything would be wonderful, because I wanted her to move in so badly. Instead, everything was horrible. At the time, we tended to blame it on her father being here, but Elizabeth was also going through grieving over her mother, so she wasn't happy. Being egotistical, I thought that I was responsible for her unhappiness and that I needed to do something to make her happy, so I kept trying to. She'd withdraw, and I'd come charging in to try to make everything okay. The harder I tried, the more she'd withdraw. It was making us both crazy.

Elizabeth: After eight years of therapy, it's okay.

Jen: She moved in in February, and in April, we went to a therapist who was wonderful. She pointed out what we were doing. She zeroed in on our stuff, and once we broke that cycle, we were okay.

Elizabeth: Driving to therapy the first time, we looked at one another and said, "We don't care what she says, we're going to stay together."

Jen: I think we were both kind of panicking, thinking that she was going to say, "This is never going to work out. Call it quits." We didn't care what she said; we would make it work.

We both wanted the same things. I think that wanting the same things from life is probably more important than that 'in love' feeling. What we have that's the strongest is that our relationship's real important to us, and our children are real important to us. Even though we haven't said 'forever,' we've been committed enough so that even from the beginning, when it seemed like it was going to be impossible, we were committed to trying to work it out. We've had some bumps along the way, and we went to therapy again four years ago, right after we got Anne--a major change.

Elizabeth: It was my desire to have children, so we started inseminating. We did that for almost a year--inseminated, fertility drugs. The last straw for me was having a biopsy. When that came back normal, the doctor said, "There are other things we could do," and I said, "No. I'm done."

Jen: It was funny, because it was like something that Elizabeth had to go through to get to the point of saying okay to adoption. I've felt like adoption was the way to go from the start, but she really wanted to go through the process of having a baby.

Adoption was just not acceptable to her, and probably at that time, anything but a white baby was unacceptable to her. Then this decision to adopt a black child seemed to evolve. You could see it; it was like she changed.

Elizabeth: I had no control over it. I didn't feel out of control, but things were just moving along, and it was okay.

Jen: It was just happening the way it should.

206

Elizabeth: And Anne took exactly nine months to get here.

Jen: From the time we were approved.

Elizabeth: So I said, "She was for us."

Jen: We both felt like she was ours, right from the start. It was instant when you saw her.

Elizabeth: She just nuzzled right in. She was only three weeks old, and it was just real natural. I was real concerned when we adopted Charlie, though, because he was two and a half months old, and his birth mother had him for a while, and then he went to a foster home. At this foster home, they were even considering adopting him. The day I met them at the office, I was sitting there waiting for Charlie, and I thought, "Oh, my God, here's this baby; he's attached to this foster mother, and I'm going to come and take him, and he's going to be crying. She walked in with him, and I looked at him, and I said, "Charlie," and he came to me, did not cry, just hugged me. It was amazing. I brought him home, and there was Anne and Jen's family. He took his nap. It was just like another day. He slept through the night the first night and never had a problem.

Jen: It seemed difficult to get the adoption at the time, but looking back, I think we had a pretty easy time of it.

Elizabeth: Jen called the adoption agency and asked if they adopted to gay people. They said they did not discriminate. However, they had no control over what would happen once other agencies got the information. So I said, "I don't want to take the chance." During the process, there was this one agency in Florida who said, "We have a child, but you will have to move out of your home."

Jen: Meaning, she'd have to leave me--even though she never was asked if she was a lesbian, and it never came up. They just didn't like the fact that she had lived with me for a period of time. She'd have to live alone to have the child.

Elizabeth: I said, "No, thank you." My caseworker was wonderful. She said, "I don't blame you. I just had to let you know that there was a child there and give you the opportunity to refuse." During the process, when my caseworker interviewed Jen, she said, "I'm sorry, but I have to treat you as a couple." I didn't have a problem going along with it. Jen was included in the whole process. There was never a time when she was left out.

I'm 'Mom,' and Jen's 'Jen,' because I can't imagine being five, six years old and in school and having two moms and then to be black, but there are times when Anne will call Jen 'Mama Jen.' At day care, people refer to us as Anne's parents. I just get real concerned when they're out in the world, and we can't protect them as much.

When I went to Anne's day care, Jen and I both went. We had an interview there, and I said, "I'm Anne's mother, and I share Anne with Jen." That's all. Jen, on the other hand, will go right out and say, "We're a couple."

I don't think that I need to go around and tell people about my personal life. Although people may be accepting of that to our face, I don't want to put Anne in a situation where she could be vulnerable when we're not there. So leave some doubt, and if they want to ask, they will.

She refers to us as her parents, but she'll still ask about her daddy, especially at day care. Daddies come to pick their kids up, and that's real hard for them, but we've talked about it. I say,

"No, you don't have a daddy," and that's fine with her. It's just when kids are being dropped off or being picked up, I think she wonders about it.

Jen: She thinks it would be pretty neat to have a daddy, but she can mention something like that that's just a fleeting thought, and we'll mull it over for days. It's gone from her right after she's said it. She doesn't care, but we care.

Elizabeth: We're on the phone to psychologists. Anne's going to have to deal with being adopted. Then to be adopted to a family with two women, without a father, and with the stresses that go along with being black, I get real upset.

Jen: When we look at Anne and Charlie, though, I think both of us see two kids that are more confident than either of us have ever felt. Anne will walk into a room, and it's like she owns the room. Any place she walks into, she knows she has a right to be there and that she's queen of the hill.

****

Jen: During my first relationship, I used to say, "Well, I'm not a lesbian; I just happened to fall in love with this woman." But I was really kidding myself, because all of my real emotional attachments have been to women. I suppose there may be some man out there that I could have a real emotional attachment to, but I certainly haven't met him, and I'm not looking. I'm clearly attracted to women.

I don't know how old I was--probably eight or nine--when I said something to my mother about the woman that I marry. She said, "Oh, don't talk like that; God will punish you." I think that was the only thing she could think of to say, but it stuck in my mind. My mother says that she knew from the time that I was just a baby, and she worried about it. I think when it came down to it, they wanted their children to be happy and to be who they are. They're very supportive, but I think they wanted them to have the easiest life they could have.

I wouldn't have chosen to be a lesbian if I had a choice, but I've been very lucky that I have the kind of life that I would have wanted. Even though Elizabeth won't say forever, I feel very committed to her and to our family, and that's pretty much what I want from life. When I was a little kid, I probably knew I wanted that but couldn't imagine how that would ever come to be, but it has.

Elizabeth: I know that this is it. I'm happy in this relationship. I'm not looking for anything else.

Jen: I'm glad you said that.

Elizabeth: But when I'm asked, "Which one would you be attracted to?" I'm attracted to men. I don't know if it's just a physical attraction. I guess I'm in the middle.

Jen: Elizabeth's told me that if something ever happened between us, she wouldn't be with another woman.

Elizabeth: It's interesting. Years ago, I went to this conference, and they read this statistic that said, "One out of ten will be gay." I thought, "Wow, there are ten of us in my family; I wonder which one." I never, never thought that it could be me. I always feel uncomfortable putting the label on myself, though. It puts restrictions on, and I don't like that.

Alone

I'm alone.
Within myself I've existed only to myself.
I've known care and gentleness
Only from within the inner depths.
I've known my thoughts
And have tried to understand.

I'm alone.
Am I too much the child
And less the man
To say... "I'm scared."

-- Gordon Barker

PART 5

Anna and Nancy
John
Chris
Steven and Henry
Maggie and Thelma
Sidney
Pete and Terry
Emma
Hank

Anna and Nancy

Anna: People who don't understand what "gay" is have all kinds of crazy ideas about what gay people must be like. You hear this absurd stuff, like a heterosexual person who can't understand how a lesbian couple could raise a "normal child," especially if it's a girl. "Are you going to raise her to be a lesbian?" We have friends who are living in gay relationships, who have children, and their children are just like everybody else's kids.

People think that someone who is gay is out there to pick people up off the streets and to have these intense sexual episodes that don't involve any emotional commitment to people.

Nancy: That's ridiculous. I really am amazed that other people try to define what gay is for me. I'm more than my sexuality.

Anna: As if they know how you are in your relationship, just because you are homosexual. They're way off base.

Nancy: You get the same continuum in gay life as you do in heterosexual life: the pick-up in the bar to the homebody or the committed relationship.

Anna: We've been together twelve years--hopefully, forever. Before that, I was in the South for seven years while I completed graduate school. When I moved there from the Midwest, I was married. My husband had come home from Vietnam with serious problems related to exposure to Agent Orange. He should have gotten well, but it didn't happen that way. It just kept getting worse. He lived for six years and then died. That was a really hard time, but I had a lot of support from my classmates and my family. That was sixteen years ago, and to this day I have a wonderful relationship with my in-laws.

After my graduate program, I came to Boston and worked in a big teaching hospital. I stayed there almost five years, walked through the door every morning, and looked at Nancy sitting at the front desk.

Nancy: I was raised a Catholic and always wanted to be a nun. I was just out of seminary and wanted to go into pastoral care, so they sent me to Massachusetts for my first assignment. I remember my mentor; she was great and an important person to me. One day she brought me upstairs to pediatrics and introduced me to Anna.

I don't remember the first time I met a lot of people, but I remember the first time she introduced me to Anna. I remember what she looked like and her long hair. We didn't spend any amount of time together, and it wasn't love at first sight--sorry to burst your bubble, dear--but I went to the talks the nurses were giving to educate myself, and I went to Anna's lectures.

I worked on the information desk, and she would come through every morning at eight o'clock in her pink raincoat. If she didn't say hello, I'd be upset. I wasn't conscious of what was going on. It was just: "Oh, Anna came through the door; she didn't say hello"--not putting it together, but always noticing. Another thing: she always called me Nancy, which I liked; she never called me "Sister Nancy."

Anna: I wasn't conscious of that either. I never did that with any of the others, but I know I never addressed her with her title--not even the first time I met her. I always called her Nancy.

It was a sense of familiarity, and it wasn't a conscious decision; but Nancy was the only one.

Nancy: I had covered pediatrics, which was a short-stay type of floor and I had attachments to the children. We were very close. There was a sense of community, and I really grieved these little kids. I was in the hall one day. Anna stopped me and said, "You work in pediatrics, don't you, Nancy?" I said I did, and she asked, "Will you do me a favor?" I said, "Yeah, why?" She said, "Well, there's a little girl down in oncology who was diagnosed with a brain tumor today."

Anna: I said, "Could you go see her family? This is going to be tough."

Nancy: I think the blood drained out of me. I was so angry at her, I could have killed her. I went downstairs to the chapel, and I was telling God I was really pissed. "Why did you do this to me? Why do I have to go up there? I don't know what I'm going to say. I know the minute I see that kid, I'll become attached to her," and on and on.

Then I felt the response to my prayer: that I needed to face this situation. I went back upstairs and walked into the little girl's room. There she was in this big bed. It seemed enormous compared to her little white body with long brown hair and big blue eyes. She was so scared. Her mom and dad weren't there yet. I stayed with her, but I was afraid of her. I was afraid of loving her, afraid of her pain, afraid of her dying. She was afraid of me, too.

Later, I started to see her family, and Anna was very involved in that. That was our connection--this little girl. That was when we started spending time together.

Anna: It was a time of us building together. Because of our connection with this child, Nancy and I had a reason to be out of the building together, outside of the confines.

Nancy: It wasn't planned. It just happened, and that's when other things started to happen.

Anna: This really is kind of remarkable. I had some experience with a healing priest in the community. The little girl's family, while involved with traditional approaches to treating their child, were interested in anything they could do that was in addition to that, and they asked about a church or some special place we could take her to help with the healing from a spiritual point of view. I knew this priest had services for healing in a very active parish. It was a regular service, held once a month or once every other week.

I told them about this, and they decided to go. So Nancy and I went to the church that night. There was a lot of music with chanting. Then the healing priest, a channel for the healing energy of God, came around and touched people during the service. It's typical for those people to fall, just absolutely without reserve, flat on the floor. It's just WHAM, WHACK, flat against the floor.

I was concerned about this child, because she had low blood counts. If she was standing up in front of the pew and had this experience, she might hit her head on that wooden pew and have serious trouble. If that happened, I wanted to catch her.

So Nancy and I sat directly behind her and her family. The priest was coming around from behind and up the aisle toward us. Nancy and I were standing there on the end of the aisle with the child in front of us, and we were singing. When the priest came to us, he looked right at Nancy and I. He doesn't touch everybody, of course; but simultaneously, with his two hands, he reached up and touched each of us right on the forehead. In the same instant, both of us just went WHACK against the pew and couldn't move.

In that instant, a surge of energy went through our bodies. It was the spirit of God through this priest to the two of us. He didn't often touch two people at the same time, and Nancy hadn't known about it in advance. This was the first time she'd ever gone, but we were both just lying there, conscious, but limp.

Nancy: Most of the time, he was just taking one hand and going up to individual people, but he looked right at us. He had the most penetrating, prayerful eyes. He just looked and focused on us. Then something went through us.

Anna: That was an intense spiritual experience, and it was our beginning. After that, we became aware of and began experiencing our relationship.

Nancy: One night I was studying in my office, and I got a phone call. The first thing I thought was, "Oh, God, Mary died"; but it was Anna, and she just wanted to talk. As we talked, I thought, "She's going to want me to come over," and I was determined that if she did, I was going.

Anna: She wasn't allowed to do that. She told me she was going to come, but I knew she couldn't. They weren't allowed to go out in the evening.

Nancy: I had to ask permission, and I didn't have a car.

Anna: I lived about 25 miles away.

Nancy: I don't know what got into my head. I told her I'd call her back, and I went over to the main house for permission. There was a nun there who was visiting. She asked,

"Why doesn't she come here?" I said, "Here? In the library? If somebody's upset, I don't think they're going to want to come here and talk." Then she said, "How are you going to get there?" I said, "I think she has a car, so she can come get me," and finally she said, "Go ahead." Anna came and picked me up. When we got back to her house, we just sat there, and I knew something was happening.

Anna: Well, you kept looking at me in the car and I thought, "What is she looking at?"

Nancy: You said, "I hope you're not going to be sorry about this," and I said, "I guarantee you, I won't be." I didn't really know what I was saying. It wasn't conscious.

We got to her house, and she had a fireplace. I love fireplaces, so I said "Oh, would you light that?" and she did. We were sitting there talking, and I took off my veil.

Anna: She's not allowed to do that.

Nancy: No. But I didn't know what the difference was. It was great. I felt so relaxed. I hadn't felt that "at home" in years. I had been seriously considering leaving the convent before this, because I was unhappy.

I liked my work. I liked my role as a sister, but I didn't get enough nurturing and support for myself. It was like I was an empty shell. That's how I felt, anyway, because I didn't get anything back from the community that was supposed to support me. They had a lot of rules; and while it's not like that in every community, in this particular house, I felt like I had ten mothers. At one time or another, I wasn't living up to someone's expectations. I'd go to the hospital, and I was a respected adult. People came to me with their concerns. I'd go back home, and I was five years old again. It was awful. It was frustrating, and I wanted out. I only realized afterward how depressed I was.

Anna and I were talking about this, and I got quiet. Bold old Anna said, "Why don't you come over here?" Well, don't ask me twice. I went over and we started hugging. I ended up kissing her. Then she said, "What do you want to do with the time we have left?" I had to be back at 11 o'clock. I didn't know what she wanted to do, but I said, "I guess I want to do the same thing you do." So, we ended up making love. I don't know how they didn't notice any difference in me the next day.

Anna: I woke up the next morning, and I wasn't really sure I hadn't dreamed it. I thought, "Is this real?" Then I looked down beside me, and there were Nancy's medals on the floor. So I knew it really did happen.

Nancy: I had to tell them I was leaving. I didn't know what I was going to do. I definitely didn't want to go to my parents' house. I had friends in New York. I knew that I could stay with them until I got myself on my feet. Anna and I were having dinner at Burger King, of all places, and talking about it.

Anna: It was all we could afford.

Nancy: I said, "Well, I guess I have these options," and she said, "You can't go there. Why don't you move in with me?" I said, "I never thought you'd ask." Then she said, "Do you want to marry me?" I thought that was the funniest thing I'd ever heard, so I said, "Sure, I'll marry you," and we decided that we would try it.

Everybody in our house knew that I was leaving. I talked individually with each sister. I was and I wasn't honest with them. I was honest, in that I told them that I really wanted to be married, but they didn't know what that meant to me. I always felt like I'd deceived them. Then I packed my things, said good-bye to the sisters, and wearing my habit, walked out the door. Two of them drove me to Anna's house. They brought in the trunk, sat down and visited. Then I went into another room, changed my clothes, came back, handed them the habit, and they left.

John

I'm a recovering alcoholic. I probably wouldn't be alive today, if I hadn't stopped drinking. I owe my sobriety to God--a power greater than myself. My life wasn't saved, and I wasn't taken out of the gutter to discover my sexuality, to have somebody tell me that God doesn't want me to be gay. It's just not the way it happened. I tried to stop drinking a hundred times, and until I surrendered, I was never able to stop. What's happening to me is entirely out of my control.

I knew when I hit college that I was gay. I couldn't verbalize it, because I was still dating women at the time. I joined a fraternity, but I was drinking very heavily. I started drinking as soon as I could, probably when I was about seventeen, but I didn't really kick in until I got to college. I became a daily drinker, because it allowed me to numb that whole side of me. I was having some very brief affairs with men then, and it was wonderful, but I was still dating a woman, who I loved very much, and I was also having sex with her. It just didn't work. I drank and drank and drank. I got through college, broke up with this woman, met another woman, who I also fell in love with, and she left me. I suspect that she probably thought I was gay, but I was also drinking a lot. By that point, I was also lying a lot. I was living two lives. I was creating this facade of somebody very materialistic--a fake, high-flying sort of person--because I wasn't comfortable with who I was.

223

Then I met Karl--the first man that ever paid any attention to me. I was 23 and right out of college. We were together for three years, but our relationship was in the closet. When he left me, it was like it never existed. I was in pain and nobody ever knew, because we had never told anybody that we were together; we were just roommates. We had lots of friends. We looked great together. We were that age where you could just be roommates, and there were all sorts of women around. I've since found out that people suspected, but nobody ever confronted us on it, because we passed. Karl was very funny, and I was very likeable, and they'd turn their head the other way. But when we split up, I couldn't share that with anybody, and it was like that three years of my life didn't exist.

Then my drinking got worse, and I was drinking heavily every night. I had a very serious car accident, and things started to deteriorate at work. I was starting to call in sick, and I was traveling a lot. I was keeping myself very busy, so I couldn't deal with my sexuality or the pain that I was going through.

Two years went by, and I found myself at a men's noon meeting. It's an AA meeting that meets Monday through Friday. A friend of mine at work--actually who worked for me--said that he was an alcoholic and needed to go to noon meetings. I said, "That's okay; I support that; you can take the time to go." One day I said, "Can I go with you?" I don't know why I said that. I had been thinking that I might have a drinking problem, but I don't know why it was that day. I went, and although I didn't stop drinking immediately, it was shortly thereafter.

I did everything they told me to do, except stop drinking. You're supposed to have a home group, and you're supposed to go to a meeting a day, and you're supposed to read the Big Book, and you're supposed to get a sponsor, and you're supposed to stop drinking. Well, I wasn't going to let go of it that easily.

One Sunday morning, I was supposed to meet my sponsor, who has been a very important part of my life. A friend of mine came up the Saturday night before, and I ended up drinking and getting very drunk. I called my sponsor Sunday morning, and I lied, "I've had out-of-town guests. I'm not going to be able to make it, but I will meet you Monday." I started the old patterns again, starting to lie to this person who had offered to help me. I met him at the meeting on Monday night, and I said, "I have something to tell you." I was very somber about it. I said, "I drank this weekend, and I got drunk." I was expecting him to say, "Oh, you're a jerk. What a loser. I'm not going to work with you." He looked me straight in the eye, and he chuckled a little, and he said, "Of course you did. You're an alcoholic." I haven't had a drink since. It was the first time that it made sense, that of course I drank and I got drunk, because I was an alcoholic. It all happens in its own time, I guess.

One of the prerequisites about getting sober is that they strongly recommend if you're single, no major changes, including that you do not get into any major relationships, that you do not do anything for the first year, except learn to take care of yourself and just don't drink. I said to my sponsor, "Thank God." That was the answer to my prayers. There wasn't this pressure to be dating, so there was no pressure to deal with my sexuality. My first anniversary, I said to him, "Oh, do I have to start dating now?" And he said, "You don't have to, if you don't want to. If you want to take another year, go ahead, take another year." So I took another year.

I was abstinent for about four years. I thought that was important to discovering who I was, because I so desperately wanted to be straight. I could have done it. I could never have been straight, but I could have lived that model, and I could have pleased everybody else except myself.

I was going to a bazillion meetings. Recovery started to help me learn to be myself, and I started to feel comfortable about that. Meanwhile, my career was getting much better. I had gotten promoted, and I was very politically involved. I was feeling comfortable in some of the other things that I was doing, and it became time to start looking at my sexuality. I needed to find people that were more like me. It was one thing to be in a room with recovering alcoholics, but I knew that there was a piece that was missing. I needed to meet other people that were like me in my sexual orientation, which meant gay men and lesbians.

Growing up, I was never quite sure who I was. I remember nodding myself to sleep, just sort of shaking my head back and forth saying, "Where are all the people just like me? I'm going to be alone all my life." I knew that I was different, and I knew that I was--I didn't know the word 'gay,' and I would never utter the word 'queer.' Then a year ago, I was sitting in a men's meeting with recovering alcoholics--all recovering gay men--and there were all people just like me. Finally. All working on their stuff, all at a different place, all putting their best foot forward, struggling with life, struggling with addiction, and struggling with being gay. And being happy, because they finally found where they fit. I had found the people I had been looking for all my life.

I came out to my parents the week before Christmas of last year. It was a very traumatic thing. I was sitting in the living room, and I said, "Dad, can we go for a walk?" He said, sure. So

226

we went for a walk, and I was telling him about recovering, because at that point I was almost four years sober, and part of my recovery is to get rid of all the secrets. I said, "I have one big secret left that I've been keeping from you," and I started to cry. He said, "What's the matter, John?" I hugged him, and he hugged me back, and I said, "Dad, I'm gay." He just patted me on the back, and he kissed me on the cheek, and he said, "That's okay, I love you anyway." And he just loves me.

I told my mother, and she accepted it and was very wonderful about it. The only remark she made that concerned me was she said, "I really feel bad that you're never going to be happy." I just said, "Well, we'll see about that."

I have a relationship, now, with a man who I'm beginning to love and who loves me, who can provide me with the physical and spiritual nurturing that I've always wanted, who can draw the line between physical and spiritual nurturing and sex, because they're not the same thing. We haven't had sex yet. We've been together for two months, and we talk about it, but we just hold each other, and that's very powerful, because that's all I ever wanted. There's time to smell the roses, so to speak. It would be so easy to skip by that in the excitement of it all. To take the time to do that is also making me whole and complete.

The other wonderful thing about this relationship and the lessons that I'm continuing to learn is that I will never again accept anything less than that. I always wanted it to happen, but I never thought it was possible, because I was gay. I didn't think I deserved it, but I do deserve it. It's very powerful, and it's such a struggle, because those are not the models that you see or the things you were taught.

Now, I'm living life, and I'm happy, and it's working. I have changed so much in the last eighteen months, people don't even recognize me. I get so overwhelmed, I can't believe how lucky I am. I'm so grateful to be alive, to have me, and there's no going back. There's this whole attitude thing that gay men have. It's that wall: I'm not going to let you in, so you can't hurt me; I'm going to pretend you don't exist. Then, there's this beauty thing: I'm going to be well-built and look like a million bucks, and you can't "kick sand in my face." It works, but the problem is you shut people out. You don't let anybody in, but you can't get out, either, and it's terrible. People do it in different ways. People do it behind businesses; they do it behind educations; they do it behind automobiles, clothing, whatever works to feel better about yourself or to hide the pain or to not feel the pain. It keeps them alive.

I think that what people are going to find is that as it becomes safer and safer to come out, the people who are passing now won't need to any more. I'm meeting men now that if I met them on the street or saw them anywhere, I wouldn't have a clue, and I'm sensitive to it. It's really wonderful, because what's happening is that those people are going to make the stereotype disappear. There are people I know in our community who are closet cases that act out in the park. They are married with children, have big positions, and are very unhappy, but they've made the choice. I only know because of the circle of people that I travel in. I think it's too bad, but you have to be ready to come out. In order to do it, you really have to love that part of yourself, and you just can't all of a sudden do it.

I've only been "out" for about eighteen months, and I find myself having very little patience for people who aren't out, being very condescending, feeling better than them, but I never want to

228

forget where I came from--that I was scared, afraid of being discovered, drinking, unhappy, self-loathing, never quite sure what corner to turn, and living a lie. I was given a second chance to live my life. I have no idea what's in store for me, but I know that I'm prepared for it now and that I'm going to do it as a gay man. Nothing short of that.

Chris

I'm far more comfortable with myself now than I have been before. What's nice about it for me is that my sexual orientation is only one aspect of me. It's not a focus point for the people that I work with or for my social friends. It's not like, "Chris is gay"; it's just one of a whole lot of other things that define who I am. That feels comfortable and right. I'm fortunate to live and work in an environment where I can be open. I can have a picture of my lover on my desk, and people don't say, "Oh, my!" We get invitations as a couple, and people are, by and large, comfortable and accepting of that.

Until recently, I was able to be open with everyone else, but not with my family or with the community where I grew up. That community was very important to me, but I had to get away from it, because I couldn't be myself there. I had this dissonance, where I would be here and have a very comfortable, open life; then I'd go back to Pennsylvania, and I just wouldn't talk about whole aspects of my existence because it might upset someone.

Over the years, I've come out to various people in my family: first to a sister, then a brother, then another brother, and then my mother and another brother. Finally, I had to confront Dad, which was not, and continues not to be easy. My father's reaction was, "Just stop doing this," as if I could. He said to me, "Have you thought about getting counseling for this?" I said, "No," and he said, "I think I might." I said, "Well, good, I think you ought to."

231

My mother is from the school that believes, "I never want to do anything that causes me to lose communication with my children. I may not like what you do; I may not like the decisions you make, but I will always support you and love you and always be in touch with you." I think my father feels that too, but he's not someone who always communicates how he feels.

My mother came to visit several years ago, and it was a nice visit, but there was that undertone of tension I always felt when visiting them. I was afraid I might say something and then we were going to have to deal with the coming-out scene. The morning I was to take her to the airport, in our last half hour, my mother says, "So, how is your life?" and wants to have the heavy, deep, real conversation. I made a flip comment, and she says, "No, really, do you think that you'll ever marry?" I took a deep breath, and then we had a long talk, and from that time on, the tension lifted. We drove to the airport, and her plane was delayed, so we went for a cup of coffee. I had the most relaxed, honest conversation with my mother that I'd had in years. I feel much more relaxed with my family now.

For parents, homosexuality is somehow a reflection on the job they did raising their children. For my parents, it's also a reflection on their social standing. For my father, it's shaking the foundation of what he believes. He is a minister in an increasingly conservative church that has said this is wrong and sinful, and he has selectively read, out of context, Bible passages to support that point of view. He has said, although not in so many words, "I have to embrace you, because you're my daughter; but if I believe this is wrong, and now you tell me that you're like this, how can I face my colleagues and say my daughter's gay?"

232

So we, as gay people, take the blame for it, but I think it's really about how a parent feels he or she has done as a parent and how that challenges their beliefs and their expectations. I try to say, "I think you did a great job raising me. You raised me to be open to a lot of possibilities, and I'm not devastated by discovering that I'm a lesbian. I think that's a sign that you were good parents."

I have tried to make a conscious decision to live deliberately and not to hide--not to be flamboyant either, but to live honestly. I am just like anyone else. Hopefully, some day the things that parents can imagine for their children can have more possibilities. It'll not be simply, "My girl's going to grow up, marry a boy, and they're going to have grandchildren for us."

Steven and Henry

Steven: It'll be five years that we've lived together.

Henry: I hope we're in it for our lives. We still have our problems, like he's more open than I am, and that's a problem. I work at a construction company. I'm the Operations and Safety Manager. I did long haul truck driving for four years before that.

Steven: I work as a teacher's aide for handicapped children. I'm open at work, very open. But Henry can't be open at his work.

Henry: No. There's one or two who know, and I get a few comments that I've heard in the background before, but I don't let it bother me, because they all work for me. To my face, the people in the office are good about it, but people are different behind your back. Two years ago, we had a safety meeting, and I was handing out the awards; I shook one of the guy's hand and gave him his check and his pin, and I could hear from off to the right, he should have wore gloves or something like that. I just ignored it, but I remembered who said it. You can say that it don't bother you, but in the back of your mind you still think about it.

Steven: I get comments like that at work once in a while, but I speak up. Everybody there knows I'm gay.

Henry: I told my mother a couple of years ago.

Steven: She was going to get you help.

Henry: I told her over the phone and went up the next night. My stepfather just couldn't accept it, wouldn't accept it, didn't understand why. He's been around since I was ten or eleven years old, and we used to do a lot together--go fishing and stuff like that. It's kind of out of their mind now. I think they've kind of blocked it out.

Steven: They don't want to hear about it.

Henry: We used to go over there as a couple before they knew. Everything was fine. When I go over there by myself, it's, "Just don't talk about it." I think it will always be that way. Just because I told them, I'm missing out being with them, and they're missing out being with me. It's like I told my mother, I just got tired of lying and fighting, but we still could do things together as a family. I feel I was honest with them, and I'm not trying to throw it in their face. I'm the same person that they've known for twenty-seven years; I just happen to live with a man. When we first met, we used to go over there for dinner and stuff like that, but we was roommates then. I just wish my parents would wake up. It's been almost five years that Steven and I have been together, and I haven't been close to them since then.

Steven: I came out when I was probably 12 or 13. I knew for quite a while before that--probably from 8 or 9. My mother's real supportive, anyways. I ended up telling my sister and telling my mother directly afterwards. She just said it would be a hard life, and I really ought to give it thought. We talked a couple years ago, and she told me things that she was thinking at that time, like it really grossed her out and she didn't understand it and she couldn't believe it. But at the time, she was terrific. She was real supportive. My father's a different story. I didn't live with my father. They're divorced.

Henry: I knew from, I can't remember how old I was, that I was "different". Sometimes I still feel that we're "different," because of all the things that you hear, and you go out somewhere, and people just stare. But I always knew that I was more attracted to men. I got to that point, growing up through high school and everything, when all my friends were dating and I never really dated. Towards the end of high school, I started dating, but it wasn't very much. There were only a couple girls that I went to bed with.

I went through a stage where I went off trying to prove to myself that I wasn't gay. It just wasn't fulfilling feelingswise. You're supposed to go fishing and hunting, and I enjoyed some of that, too, but it's just when it came to being with somebody, I'd rather be with a man than a woman.

Then, trying to prove that I could be with a woman, I ended up with a kid. I was fifteen, and she was twenty. That was a real turmoil situation with her family. Her brothers tried to run me off the road, and she wouldn't let me see the kid, so I never attempted to. I figure some day, my daughter will want to see me. I was totally confused, because I figured this was the way my stepfather would want me. You're supposed to get married and have kids. My uncle was a role model. He was successful and had a family and everything you would want.

Even growing up in a supposedly straight life, there was always the comments. In school, they was always making gay jokes, or queer jokes.

Steven: You can tell if someone's doing it to be rotten.

Henry: But you just hear so much of it, I get sick of them. It's like when I hear them at work, I don't know if they're saying them because they have suspicions that I am or what. Why does it have to be a gay joke?

237

People identify the whole gay population with the drag queens, and that's not accurate. All most people see is what they see on TV or what they see in the paper.

It's just like people that are prejudiced against Blacks. It's no different. Everybody's people. No matter who you are, there's good and bad, and that will always be.

Maggie and Thelma

Thelma: My life right now feels very normal. I have a decent job as a child protective worker. I've been doing this kind of work, basically, for 27 years.

When I'm reviewing my past and all the years, I wouldn't want to repeat most of them up until I became involved with Maggie. When I got involved with Maggie and started seeing what a healthy relationship felt like, it was just incredible to me. I believe strongly that all of us have homophobia to some degree, because of the stigma that's attached to being gay. But since I've been with Maggie, I've really gotten away from that. I feel healthy in relationship to myself for the first time in my adult life.

Maggie: It's really fascinating, because in personality we're probably like night and day. Thelma's an extrovert; I'm a recovering introvert, but I've learned to hide it.

Thelma: I'm volatile. Maggie thinks before she opens her mouth.

Maggie: Yet, we're alike in all the little things, like enjoying the same things on vacation. We can go into Boston, walk the city streets and be happy, or we can be driving around here, and we'll both be fascinated to see where that little dirt road goes, or just throw the canoe on top of the car and go over to a stream or someplace else to explore.

Thelma: We're both avid mystery fans, but I'm the book reviewer, because I do more reading and faster reading than Maggie. I can keep my eyes open longer than three minutes when

I go to bed. So I line up books for Maggie after I've read them, if they're good. We both like sports, and we love the island where we have some land, but we don't travel well together. We've had to really work at that. Most of the things we do we don't have to even think about, but when we first started traveling together, it's a wonder we ever got from here to Long Island and back without killing each other.

I am not a good map reader. Maggie would be driving; she'd have me reading the map, and she'd be asking me a question. I'd say, "Jesus, I don't know where this road goes. I can't even find this road on the map."

Maggie: I forgot that there are map people and not-map people.

Thelma: I hate map-reading, especially when I'm in the process of doing it.

Maggie: I'm saying, "Is this the turn-off? Is it the road we're supposed to take? What lane am I supposed to be in? What lane?"

Thelma: "I don't know what lane you're supposed to be in. Just go. We'll circle around, if we have to." I don't care if we're lost. I just follow my nose, because eventually I get where I want to go.

****

Maggie: In Thelma's family, her mother used to say to her, "If you're not good, you're going to end up like your sister, Susan." Susan is a lesbian.

Thelma: My mother used to compare my sister, who's sixteen months older than I am, and me to the twins. My sister was like the "good" twin, and I was like the "bad" twin, the lesbian. When I was a sophomore or junior in high school, my mother first said the word "homosexual" in talking about Susan and made it really sound ugly. "You're going to turn out to be just like her." I thought, well, that must be the worst thing that anybody can possibly be. I can still picture the expression on my mother's face when she said that Susan was "a homosexual" and I was going to be just like her. There was such hatred in her face about the whole idea.

It was not until I was 27 that I became involved in a real lesbian relationship, but I couldn't work at that relationship, because I couldn't reconcile all the stuff I had heard at home with what could have been a good relationship.

Maggie: When I was growing up, my little sister was the blonde-haired, blue-eyed angel, and although I look at pictures and I wasn't an ugly kid, I identified myself as being an ugly duckling and a tomboy. I always felt different and very alone.

I didn't date in high school, and I only dated a little in college. That was really only because that's what you were supposed to do. It never felt right, and I always had best friends who were women. I was really into denial about my sexuality.

After college, I was visiting one of my oldest and best friends, and she came out to me. I forget how she framed it, but she said, "Martha propositioned me, and I'm really considering what to do about it. What do you think?" I said, "Well, Carol, I think whatever you decide, you'll still be my friend." When she finally came out, it was just this wonderful event in her life; she wanted everybody to know, but I was really uncomfortable with it. I can remember driving around and my knuckles getting white, thinking "Oh, my God, poor Carol, if she's a lesbian, everybody will reject her. She'll have such a hard time."

241

I continued living in my denial, until I ended up falling in love with a woman and acknowledging it, partly because she was fairly aggressive and, at the same time, very tolerant. I was involved in the relationship for two years, although we never lived together. I wasn't capable of a decent relationship at that point. Finally, I had this awful year where everything bad that could possibly happen did. Then I got mono, and the person I had been involved with decided she couldn't deal with me any more. In the spring, still fighting the mono, I saw the ad for the job here. I applied because my sister was here, I had two nephews here, and it might mean a trip to visit. Everything fell into place like it was meant to be.

****

Maggie: I'm semi-out in my job. I don't wear a sign across my forehead, but I don't hide the fact that Thelma and I are a couple. I don't watch my pronouns particularly, and I took Thelma to the president's house for dinner. He and his wife were both very gracious and welcoming. I think he knew, but he respected what I chose to share, and I was uncomfortable about sharing too much.

Thelma: I'm pretty careful about what I say to whom. There are a lot of lesbians working where I work, but even so, there's a lot of homophobia. In general, though, I'm more open than ever before in my life. I'm a human being. I love Maggie, and granted, I'm careful about the environment in which I express that love, but I think I would be in any relationship.

Maggie: I call it homophobia phobia, which can be really destructive. When I came out, I was so afraid of the reaction of close friends of mine that I distanced myself. When I finally had to tell them, it was fine, and they had known. The fear of their reaction was what was damaging, which is why I decided to come out here.

Thelma: You come to terms with being a lesbian when you finally stop struggling against it.

Maggie: It's all a pattern of breaking through denial.

Thelma: When you're raised in a homophobic society, though, you're very conscious of the fact that all of a sudden, people who were your friends until you put a label on yourself don't know you any more, and they don't want to know you. Why does just saying the words change a relationship?

Sidney

I've been HIV-positive for the last seven years. I have no symptoms and a good T-cell count. I get acupuncture, which I think is excellent. It's very relaxing. I do a lot of things to keep my stress level low. I think that helps a lot. I make a lot of job decisions and who I'm going to have in my life based on stress level and treating myself well that way. I like this life a lot better than any of my previous ones.

As a kid, I never did have any friends, except I had a friend in fifth grade. I remember her especially, because I had a crush on her. She was my first and last friend. I didn't socialize very well.

I was very close to my brother, who had Downs Syndrome. When I was about ten, just one day out of the blue, without any warning, they told us that he was going to live in an institution. I later found out that when my sister was fifteen and she ran away from home and was put in a foster home, she reported my parents for abusing my brother. I guess they proved that he had been being abused and pulled him from the home, but we weren't told any of this. It was very devastating for me when that happened. I started drinking shortly after that, and I started stealing. When I'd babysit or something, I'd steal booze.

I got out of high school and went to work in the fish factory. I moved in with some people who had a party house; we spent all our time partying. I would get up in the morning and go to work with a thermos full of booze and a bag of pot. I cut my finger once really bad and got blood poisoning. I was excited because it meant I got three days of worker's comp. I could stay home and party. I was a virgin until I was eighteen, but after that, when I drank, I'd have sex with anybody. It didn't matter.

Eventually, I got pregnant. I didn't know who the father was, because I used to have black-outs when I drank. This woman I was renting a room from used to say, "If you ever need help, come talk to me." I had no clue what she meant. I planned out my suicide. As a last ditch effort, I decided to ask this woman for help. She took me to a woman's counseling place. Within a week, I was in AA and haven't had a drink since. Next month, it will be nine years that I've been sober.

I had the baby and put him up for adoption when he was born. The delivery was a beautiful thing. The doctors wanted to put me to sleep, but I said, "No way, I want to see this thing." I'm real grateful that I did, because now, with the HIV thing, I've chosen not to have any more children, and I'm really grateful that I had the experience.

After the baby was born, I hooked up with the guy who infected me with HIV. I left him and then met my husband. I tested negative but six months later tested positive. Two months later, I got married. My husband is negative. He was tested a year ago, and he was still negative.

I went into the marriage open about being bisexual, but the last year we were married, we had a lot of difficulties. I never really knew if it was that I was HIV-positive and could kill him, or that I didn't necessarily like being with a man. A lot of the conflict around my sexuality is also that I've been traumatized by men. When I finally made the decision to leave, we were struggling.

I felt terrible about hurting him, but I've never felt better in my whole life than I've felt since I made that decision. All that turmoil is gone. I said, "This is it. I'm out of the marriage. I've decided I'm a lesbian." It's just an incredible feeling of freedom, to just be myself. I haven't regretted the decision since I made it.

I'm very "out" now. There are certain times when I decide not to mention it, because it's not always necessary to wave a flag and say, "Here I am," but for the most part, I am completely out. I think that has to do with spending ten years in turmoil over it. I think it also has to do with being in recovery and learning in recovery that you're as sick as your secrets. The long coming-out process that I've had with HIV is a very similar situation. So now I've been out for a year.

I love the job that I'm at now. I'm able to be open about being a lesbian and open about being HIV. I mentioned that I was HIV in the job interview, because I had worked in a boarding home for people with head injuries before, and when they found out that I was HIV-positive, all of a sudden my job performance just wasn't very good any more. I didn't want to go through that again, so I figured I'd say it right up front in the interview. I don't want to be hired somewhere and then let go or forced to quit because of that. I don't want to deal with the stress of being discriminated against.

Pete and Terry

Pete: Terry and I got married, but neither one of us wore a dress. As you can tell, we are not flamboyant. That's not our thing, but we got married in September of '83.

Terry: We're going to renew our vows again this year, on our tenth anniversary. Back then, we did it in our home and had a few friends over. Now, everybody I work with is considering going to the wedding, and they're all straight couples.

Pete: We even had our rings made, because something that's made will be something that no one else has and that says a little bit about us.

The interesting thing with Terry and I is that, like a lot of people who have been together for a while, we answer each other. I'll be sitting in the car and I'll think, "Geez, you know, I really want to go look at this antique chair," and all of a sudden, he'll say, "Do you want to go look at that antique chair?" Then we'll just look at each other. We do that all the time.

I was married before. I married my high school sweetheart while I was in the service, but it was a really bad situation. I had gotten out of boot camp and gone to Florida for school. I dated some men while I was there, but nothing very serious. I finally said to myself, "Enough is enough. I can't live this lifestyle. I can't have a career in the service and take the chance of losing that career."

I started writing my girlfriend back home. We had broken up after high school, but she wrote back. One day I just said, "I really do love her. I know I love her." I did, but I think it was more like a friend. It was more acceptable to be married to a woman, have the little white house with the picket fence, the dog, the cat, and 2.5 children. So that's the route I decided to go. To my dismay, it was not a very good idea.

We were married in September 1981, and while I couldn't quite figure out what was going wrong, we kept trying. We were married for five months, and then I went to Iceland for six months. While I was gone, her brother got her involved in drugs. I came back to a person who I didn't know, who was addicted to cocaine, speed, acid, and smoking marijuana. She had an "I-don't-care" attitude and was mean to me. It got progressively worse.

I was also fighting with myself for being gay, because I knew I was gay, and I was trying to change. I was trying to be accepted, and the only way to be accepted was to be married.

Finally, I said, "I tried, but I can't deal with this any more. If I have to go through the rest of my life lonely, that's the way it's going to be. Enough is enough."

Terry: I had gotten out of high school and started working. My father was disappointed because I didn't go to college, but I didn't want to go. I just wanted to work. I met this girl. We went out, had a good time together, and she got pregnant, so we ended up getting married. It was bad from Day One, real bad.

We were off and on all the time, before my son was even born. When he came along, he was like a godsend to me. I had someone to hold on to. I knew then that I was gay, and I didn't want to be married; but I had a little boy who needed me, and I was like mother and father to him. My wife and I separated, and then we got back together again; she got pregnant again, and I had a little girl. After that, it was like, I'm stuck here. I adore my kids. I hate their mother, but I adore my kids.

This went on and on and on. I started losing a lot of weight. I got bleeding ulcers. I thought I was on the verge of a breakdown. I was very up-front with my doctor. I told him my feelings, and he came right out and told me, "Get a divorce. Get on with your life," but I couldn't because of the kids. They *were* my life, but every night was a fight.

After I met Pete, I was getting so torn, because I'd see him and then go home and fight. The only thing that saved me was that she worked nights. So I'd go home, get the kids dinner, play with the kids, bath time, bed time, and have a quiet hour; then she'd get up, rant and rave, and go to work. She'd be out of the house until seven o'clock the next morning. By the time she came home, I had the kids up, dressed, off to day care, and I'd be out the door. So we only saw each other a few minutes a day, but every time we did, it was just miserable.

One night I was on my way home from work. I envisioned the scene at home, because I knew her mood when I left that morning. I stopped at the airport and bought her and my two kids airplane tickets. Her parents were living in Florida at the time. I called her boss and told him that there were big problems in Florida and that she had to go for two weeks. I went home, and the next morning I drove to Bangor and put all three of them on the plane, and I said, "I need this for me." Of course, we fought all the way to the airport, and the kids were all upset, not knowing what was going on. I just said, "Daddy has some things on his mind. I have to take care of them." I just needed a few days.

I took a couple days off from work. I didn't see Pete. I didn't want anyone around. I just had to think.

By the time she came back, I had applied for different jobs down toward this area and had accepted a job with the newspaper. I told her, "I'm sorry, it's not working. I am so unhappy with my life. I love my kids. I'm always going to be there for my kids. I'm not going to be around all the time, but I'll be the best weekend father that the state's ever seen," and I packed and left.

Pete and I rented an apartment, and then he had to go to Iceland again for six months. We had just moved in together, for maybe about a month when he left. That was good. It gave me time to decide whether to go back to my old life or to get divorced while he was gone, so that my life would be clean when he came home.

It was hard. I was getting pulled by everybody. No one would understand me. Finally, I said, "That's it." I got divorced and had the kids every weekend. When Pete got home, we still continued to have them every other weekend, up until about six months ago when my son started working every weekend. He graduates in June, and my daughter's 15.

From Day One, we tried every legal step there was to fight for custody. Of course, the minute we'd mention that we're gay, not a lawyer would take it, and we have been through almost every law firm. Things have changed now, but what am I going to do with a son who's close to 18 and a daughter who's 15? The time that they needed me was ten years ago, and no one would help me. They all laughed at me.

Pete: We hired a lawyer and we both went every time we had a meeting. He dragged us along for almost a year and a half, charged us, and never wrote one letter. So, we went to another lawyer who said, "Report him to the bar." We reported him to the bar and never heard another word. The next lawyer who took the case did the same thing, dragged his feet, kept putting us off, giving us excuses, and didn't do a thing.

Terry: It's because every lawyer I've had knows that I'm gay, and not one of them would represent us as a gay couple and fight for us in court, not one. Pete and I have spent thousands on legal fees, and for what? It is a joke.

Pete: Granted, there are some men who are losers and who really don't care; but here's a man who really cares for his children and wants to save them from everything they are going through, and he can't.

Terry: Considering all that they went through, they're super kids. They've never been involved with drugs, and they're both 'A' students. We always kept the communication lines open.

Pete: I want the children to know that they're loved. We're here for them, no matter what, and any time they ever need us, we're just a phone call away. We do have some very happy memories. We've done some wonderful weekends with them.

Terry: Pete and I have been together for ten years--going on eleven--and have been faithful. It's not true what they say about gay men. We're not promiscuous. Most everybody we know has been that way. If you get somebody, you hold on to him.

When people think gay, they think "leather men" with the G-string. They don't see me when I go to work every morning with a suit on.

Pete: They don't see me working in a hospital, working with people, caring for people every day, and getting them up on their feet walking.

Terry: We work full time. We run a home. We have typical everything like everyone else.

Pete: I wish we could change the terms. Instead of saying "gay" and "straight," "homosexual" and "heterosexual," just say, "people." We don't like the word "lovers," because it doesn't sound permanent. We consider ourselves partners--partners for life.

Emma

I have real problems with intimate relationships. Friends I can deal with, but lovers I can't. I have no desire to. People ask me about sexual orientation, and I'm more apt to say I'm asexual than anything, because I just don't want to have sex with anybody. Most people can't understand that, but whenever I have had sex with anybody--male or female--it's been used as a method to control or to humiliate me. It has been used as a weapon to make me feel bad about myself by a man that I loved, by most of the men that I have been with, and by the one woman that I have been with. Sex to me is not a pleasant experience.

It may come partially from the fact that my mother still insists that I was found under a cabbage leaf in the back yard. My parents totally deny sex. My father just doesn't admit that it exists, and to my mother it's the worst thing that you could do. It's nasty, and nice people just don't do it. That probably explains why I'm an only child. They made a mistake, but only once.

As far back as I can remember, I've been different. I often thought God had made a mistake in my anatomy. I just didn't understand why I was made wrong. I was the wrong sex, and I had been given to the wrong parents. God screwed up-- didn't give me the right equipment and *certainly* didn't give me the right parents.

Another thing that separated me from the other little girls was that I was never going to be married. I knew that. It's not something I consciously thought about, except that when they were playing wedding, I didn't want to play. It didn't relate to me, to who and what I was.

I've always enjoyed the physical beauty of living beings-- trees, flowers, and especially animals. Give me a nice looking Morgan horse to look at or a nice looking cat or dog, and it's something that I can sit and look at for hours.

Men and women are both beautiful to me. It isn't the fact that one is more attractive than the other. Growing up, I knew I was supposed to like boys, and I knew I wasn't supposed to like girls, but I couldn't understand why. That liking was just there. It was part of me.

Somebody asked me one day, "Do you define yourself as a lesbian?" Why do I have to define myself within the confines of sexual orientation? Why do we have to be homosexual, bisexual, or heterosexual? Why can't we just be sexual? Why can't we just be human? I enjoy the beauty of both women and men. I enjoy the company of men and women. I define myself as a human being.

Hank

To start from the beginning, I think that I was probably as young as five or six when I first noticed that I wasn't exactly like everybody around me. I knew that I was more attached socially and psychologically to my male friends than I was to my female friends. I felt like that put me out of the main line, because even at that age, there's a lot of taunting and the boys going out and pulling the girls' pigtails and stuff like that. For me, I didn't want to pull the girls' pigtails; I wanted to yank on the arm of the guy next to me.

It was obvious that somehow I was differently aligned, and I think that, because I felt the difference personally, everybody around me also did. I had already begun the alienation process, where one, I felt different; two, other people felt I was different; and three, they and I treated me that way. So there was a separation of me from my peers at the ripe age of five or six. That got worse and worse and worse. By the time I was in the eighth grade, I was totally alienated from my peers.

The reasons for that alienation had to do with the growing perception among the people that I was growing up with that I was queer. There was a mutual alienation--they made fun of me, and I walked away from them. It was a two-way street. I don't want to paint the world as being ugly and mean. These people certainly pushed me away because I was different, but I think that if I had fought that, I could have come back, probably as much as 75% of the way. They wouldn't have pushed me completely out of the circle, but I let them do it. The reason for that, I think, is because I bought, hook, line, and sinker, the societal view of the gay man as being an outlaw socially and sexually and being somehow tainted, dirty, and immoral.

I would guess that I identified myself as being queer (at the time, 'gay' wasn't a word; it was 'queer') when I was old enough to have an erection. Then I knew I was queer, because I would get an erection when I looked at other boys naked. If there was a picture book around that had artistic pictures of men in jock straps and women scantily clothed, I would become stimulated whenever I looked at the men.

I got out of high school, and then something really strange happened. I went into college, I was in a dormitory situation, and I bonded. I had three roommates the first year in college, and I bonded to them and to a bunch of other friends--all male. The whole group was essentially asexual, but I really liked the contact. That was a great time of life for me--complete turn-around from the life that I was living before, where I had to seek my friends outside of my peer group and live with the alienation within my peer group. Suddenly, here I was in the middle of my peer group-- very accepted and having a great time--and then it ended.

We began to graduate from college. This group of people dissipated, and I plunged--and I mean plunged--immediately into almost total self-isolation. I severed ties with all of my friends, with all of my acquaintances, and with my family. I lived an absolutely solitary existence. I started this solitary life probably at around the age of 22, and I was 29 when I came out of it, so it was about seven years.

I was 25 years old. I would be driving down the street, and I would whisper to myself, "You're queer." It would send shock waves through me, and I'd look around the car. I was afraid that somehow that got outside the car. Somehow, even admitting it to myself in that way was so threatening to me.

I was 26 years old, and one of my co-workers asked me if I was queer. I went into absolute and total shock. I denied it vehemently and really had a lot of nasty things to say to that person for having even suggested it. I then told him that I didn't want to talk to him ever again, and I didn't for a few years. He so threatened me with that.

During those seven years came the evolution of myself, conceptually, as a gay man. I didn't want to see people; I didn't want to think sexually. In fact, I very rarely even masturbated. Then I got into my mid-twenties, and I could no longer hold down the sexual nature. I started having these dreams that were the logical extension of being with a buddy that I was really comfortable with. Rather than just kind of poking them on the arm, you put your arm around them, and you give them a hug-- intimate interpersonal contact.

From the time that I was 25 to the time that I was 29, these feelings, these dreams, these desires were building and growing in me. At about 29 years old, I was still very reclusive. I wasn't seeing my family. I wasn't going home for holidays. I was making all kinds of excuses not to see people. I was working all the time, and emotionally, I was just about at the end of my string.

My parents forced me to come down for Christmas my 29th year. As I was coming back from my parents' house, I stopped at a rest area. I had heard that that's where some gay men went to have sex. I sat in that rest area for probably twelve hours. I didn't do anything; I just sat there and watched. About a week later, I came back to the same rest area, and I sat there again for four or five hours and didn't get out of my car at all. I did this for probably three or four weeks, where I was going two or three times a week to this rest area and just watching the action.

Then one day I got out of my car, and I went up into the woods. I was up in the woods probably about ten minutes, and somebody approached me. He just walked up to me, didn't say a word, and then he dropped down to his knees, undid my pants, and started performing an act. I couldn't take that. I didn't call him any names, but I called myself a lot of names. I stormed back to my car. I was so shocked that it was probably another month, month and a half, before I went back. The next time I went back, I was ready. By then, I was so starved I entered a period of about six months to a year of fairly regular anonymous sexual contact with anybody who was willing to have that contact. It wasn't social at all. It was sexual.

One day, I met the man that I'm living with now. It felt comfortable, so rather than bringing him into the woods, I brought him home. He's stayed there ever since. It's been seventeen years. In fact, we had our anniversary this last Sunday.

I desperately needed somebody in my life. That was obvious. I was really quite close to the edge--lonely, desolate, and self-loathing. I desperately needed to be connected with the world, and it was that desperation that drove me to the rest area.

One of the things that I'm currently doing is that I recently met up with an old college pal--one of these people that I walked away from. I'm trying to renew that friendship. I walked away from him, because I was afraid of his judgment. I expected him to be mad at me for having done that to him, but there was none of it. There's ten or fifteen years here of just wasted time. His kids grew up, and I never met them. He went through a whole marriage with an ugly divorce, and I wasn't there to support him, and I could have been, if I hadn't been so stupid. I know now that I'll never throw away another friendship. Real friendships are just too precious. They're too hard to make.

Times change. Things change. I no longer need just gay friends. What I want in my life are people--real people with real emotions, real connections, and real feelings.

I didn't come out to my family until after I had met Jonathan. I'd been living with him for about two years, and then I came out to them, because I had to. They took it amazingly well, a hell of a lot better than I thought they were going to. My mother and father claim that they had not suspected. My brothers and sisters claim that they did. My father accepted it almost immediately. My mother had a hard time with it. She went through the "What did we do wrong?" stage. My father said nothing. It's the way it is, because it's the way it is.

I don't know if I'll ever feel like I'm a whole person. It's within me, but it has an awful lot to do with society's reflection back against gay people. I find, now, that I mourn the loss--the death, if you will--of my opportunities to have led a normal life as a child. It's not that I didn't have a good life, and it's not that I didn't enjoy the friends that I had who were younger and older. It's not that I didn't enjoy working all those umpteen hours, rather than dealing with real people. I did. But I understand, down deep, that there is an aspect of life, there is an appreciation of living, there is a connection "straight" people have to the world around them, particularly their connection to people around them-- their family, their friends--that I think most of them have, and frankly, I haven't a clue. I really don't know what that's like, and I feel absolutely partial because of it.

This disjointness that I feel with respect to the rest of the world isn't, in my mind, fixable. It's that total shortfall from expectancy, from normalcy, from baseline acceptance that I feel, that I just don't think is recoverable. I feel a real loss in that area. In some ways, I also grieve its loss. I would like to be "normal." That's not to say that I would like to be straight, but I would like to feel connected, and I don't think that I ever will. I will never have kids. I will never be a grandparent. I will never have those experiences,

I'm not one to cry. I guess through my life, I've been hardened, and I just don't tear up very easily. But last Christmas I was home, and I was playing with my nieces. One of my aunts came up to me, and she kind of put her arm on me, and all she said to me was, "Jesus, you know, it's really a shame that you couldn't have been a father." Right out of the blue, I just fell apart. That's what I mean when I tell you that I feel like I'm an incomplete person. The fact that I, for whatever reasons, grew up homosexual, has very much contributed to that. I can't do anything about it, and it's painful.

There are very few of us that would choose the gay experience. It's too painful. It's easier to believe that this is choice and that we are all somehow morally corrupt because of our choices. That's poppycock! It's just too frigging painful to have been a choice. I, personally, would have given anything to have grown up differently. I would have given anything to have been a straight man and to have lived a more normal life. That's not because I have any negative feelings about the homosexual experience or about people who are homosexual. It's this loss, this price that I've had to pay and that I think other people like me have had to pay, and it's just not fair. There hasn't been an open enough environment such that gays in this society have developed a healthy and correct way to live their lives.

There was a kid that was posting to the Internet a while back, and he was really in pain, talking about how he was living in a small, closed community, that he was convinced that he was the only gay person within a hundred miles of himself, and that he was going absolutely crazy--not crazy in terms of the need for sex, but crazy in terms of his self-hatred. He desperately wanted to change himself, but he couldn't. He talked about this stuff for weeks. People were trying to help him, but it's hard to do remotely. Then, suddenly, he started talking about suicide. He didn't kill himself; he's still posting, but I think that his problem isn't so much what he thinks of himself; his problem is that he fears too much what other people think of him. I think if he gave himself half a chance, he'd be comfortable with who he is. He simply has to. If the kids can get to that point before they commit suicide, then they live to be 20. But if they can't, or if they don't, they're a statistic. We are losing thousands of kids a year to this despair. That's a national tragedy.

The Lamb Released

I seek to find that inner place called "Peace"...
Yet, the "Lion" within
Is still not ready to enfold its "Lamb."
Though both strive to be embraced.

-- Gordon Barker

PART 6

Ted
Jim and Tim
Janice
Tom and Phil
Sarah and Debby
Keith
Carol
Courtland
Joe

Ted

The fact that I can love is a new discovery. The fact that I can cry and have it be a catharsis is a new discovery. The fact that I can meet individuals that society calls the dregs and identify a closeness and feel something between us that is deeper than all the plastic that surrounds us, a humanness deeper than one's sexuality, is a new discovery. The only way I can explain it is this Higher Power, something more than ourselves. You can call it God, Goddess, or Great Spirit. It's in the feeling between two people, and between yourself and nature. All the outer trappings, whether substance abuse, lying in the gutter, prostitutes, priests, great and wonderful people, when all that goes by the wayside, you come down to a little spark. I like to call it "grace."

I went through hell growing up, wondering who I was, and finally getting married. My whole life was one that was hidden, out of fear. On the outside, I was a success by anybody's standard--well-dressed, great job--but I can remember walking out of my home with a briefcase and all the trappings of success and feeling worthless inside, a nobody. I think a lot of gay people have experienced that.

I met my wife when I was 23, and we married. I love this woman. I love her for her intuition, her goodness, her intelligence, her nurturing, and for our children. Yet, there was something missing that she could not give me, nor I give to her. It's sad. It'll always be sad. There will always be a melancholy about it, and there will always be a pain. It's like ripping a vital part out of me and out of her. I can't describe the pain, but a certain amount of it will always be there.

We went through counseling, psychologists, and psychiatrists, even a nutritional biochemist. We went through hell. We had to get a lot of feelings out. We knew we had to do something. Over a period of three years, we separated, I moved in here, and we've been going to therapy. Now we're in the business of divorce. We have closed the door on a marriage and opened another one on a harmonious friendship.

I had met a young man. Our birthdays were ten days apart, and we were built alike. Over the course of six months, I became really attracted to him. I'll never forget him. I experienced something with him that I had never experienced in my life, but it was frightening. I had a wife--a wonderful woman--and we had four children.

I also had a lot of physical ailments: stomach trouble and heart trouble. Because I worked in the pharmaceutical field as a sales representative, I knew doctors that I called on as part of my job. I met one doctor who did all kinds of tests, and he thought I should have some psychiatric treatment. So I embarked on getting psychiatric help.

When I first went into the hospital, I told my wife I was having homosexual feelings. She didn't understand. We went together to talk to the doctors at the hospital, and they told us that this was a symptom of other things. "We'll clear the depression, and that will go away." I went to 16 different doctors. Neither the depression nor the homosexual feelings went away.

I got more depressed, had more hospitalization, got more shock treatments. I had nineteen electric shock treatments to change me from being homosexual to being straight. On the twentieth, I said "No."

Then I went the religious route. I called on priests. I met one priest over lunch and divulged my personal feelings. He said, "Well, why don't we make an appointment for you to come to the rectory?" Once I was there, he maneuvered me in such a way to get me upstairs to his bedroom. I freaked out. I could not say no, so I just turned and left. That was extremely disturbing. It crippled me for months. Eventually, I became disabled and lost my job. When I could no longer take the pain, I attempted suicide.

Finally, I went to see my cousin, an Episcopal priest. He is also a gay man who started out in the civil rights movement and is now a street priest. He has designed an AIDS agency to help people out in the street. He says these are his people. After spending a week with him, I came back, went to the AIDS Project, and joined the Buddy program.

I took on a 36-year-old former prisoner, IV-drug user, drug peddler, uneducated, very hard-core person. I have a college education, come from an upper middle class family, and have all the trappings of a white Anglo-Saxon Protestant, in spite of being brought up Catholic. We hit it off. I connected with him. We talked about almost everything.

I drove him back and forth to the doctor's office. He kept putting his hand on my arm and saying, "Ted, it's so good to have a buddy who's straight that I can talk to." That went on for six months. Before me, he had had three other buddies. All of them were gay men, and he had trouble with that. He was homophobic and hated gays. I'd been introduced as, "This is Ted. He lives with his wife. He has four children and five grandchildren." He had come up to my house, and my wife liked him. I figured,

"Some day I'm going to have to tell this man that I'm gay. I cannot go under this pretense any more. I am deceiving this man, and it's not fair; not just to him, but to me." My wife and I were separating, and I was moving in here.

One day, we were on the way home from the hospital and had stopped at a red light. Again, he was talking: "It's good to have a straight buddy. I hope some day, if you're ever in this position, Ted, you'll find a friend like I have in you." At that red light, I turned to him, and I said, "Joe, I have something to tell you." I looked at him, then I turned my head forward and just stared out front at the traffic light again. I said, "Joe, I'm a gay man." I could see him out of the corner of my eye. He was still for the longest time, then all of a sudden, I saw him jump around quick, and out come his hands. I thought he was going to hit me, but he put his arms around my head, drew me over to him, and kissed me. He says, "You know, Ted, nobody has ever trusted me like you do."

Today, Richard is my partner. He is younger than I am. There's 30 years difference. We've been together about a year and a half, almost two years now. I don't know what to make of this relationship, but I know that we're soulmates. I don't know how these things come about. We don't have the necessary role models, and I still get confused about the marriage vows I took with my wife.

I think my goal in life is to be self-loving, and self-respecting, so that no matter what comes along, I have something to fall back on. I believe there is something higher than us, and it's comforting to feel that.

Jim and Tim

Tim: I thought I knew Jim. You're raised with somebody all your life, the same age, and you think you know them, especially when you're twins. I can tell things about Jim, even if I'm not there. He was hurt one day coming back from a hockey game. He fell and cut himself on the hand and knocked himself out. I was at home with my wife, and we were laying on the couch watching TV. I had this uncontrollable pain in my hand. My mother called me later that night and told me that he was in the hospital.

All of our lives we shared a lot of time together and to not know he was gay, I felt betrayed, upset, hurt, angered, a lot of things. I was the last to find out, and I was very upset when I did find out.

Jim: It was hard to confront you.

Tim: He knew how I would take it.

Jim: I just know how you reacted whenever you saw someone that was gay and flamboyant. It was always very derogatory: "those faggots." We were very close growing up, and for a lot of gay people, the biggest fear is that you've failed your family. You know that everyone in your family looks up to you. It makes it really hard.

Tim: For a while, I wouldn't accept it, but he's my brother, and I love him, and what he does is his life. I've got to respect him for what he wants. If it makes him happy, then it makes me happy.

Jim does his best to spoil his nephews and nieces come Christmas and birthdays. I try to explain to my little boy not to expect to get something every time he comes up here, but Jim usually finds a way to spoil him, so when he leaves, he has something.

Jim: I think that's because I've realized that I'm not going to have kids of my own. A lot of people don't realize the sacrifice, in that sense. I'm very fortunate that my family has been supportive.

When I was with my former partner, my sister's little boys would come up, and they'd say, "We're going to go see Uncle Jim and Uncle George." That innocence of a child makes you feel good. They didn't care. They're not looking at Uncle Jim and Uncle George and thinking, "Well, they're sleeping together." To them, it was two people that they cared about and they wanted to visit, because they knew they'd get presents.

******

Jim: My whole freshman year in college, I never met anyone, because you don't know where to go. I knew there was a bar where the clientele on certain nights were gay, but I was only eighteen and under age. Gay people can't go to parties, meet other people, strike up a conversation and then maybe have a relationship. You had to know where they hang out. So, if you were gay and you wanted to meet other guys, you'd have to stumble across it, or someone has to mention, "Oh, yeah, those faggots, they're down on such-and-such."

My big awakening was when I was 21. I met this gentleman, who had a lover. He lived on a farm, and he invited me to come down for the weekend. I was a little nervous, but I went, and he introduced me to his friends. Just experiencing gay life, seeing two people who were open, who weren't trying to watch what they were saying or who they were saying it to, and who were openly showing affection, I went home after that weekend and said, "Why am I doing this to myself?" Two weeks later was spring break. I went down and spent the two weeks down there and ended up, at the end of the year, moving down there for the summer.

That was the summer my mother called and asked me. She had heard a rumor that I was living with two gay gentlemen. I never lied to her. So when she said, "Are you living with two gay men?" I said, "Yes, I am." She said, "You're not like that, are you?" I said, "Yes, I am. I didn't want this to come out over the phone, but we will sit down real soon, and we will talk about it. I don't want you to feel guilty, because it's not your fault. This is the way I am."

I remember writing my sister that summer, too. I said, "I am so happy. I've met someone." Of course, I didn't tell her it was a guy. I said, "I've met this woman. I've never been so happy." I really was. I felt good about myself, and I finally had people I could talk with and be with that were like me.

I think that's part of a second growing up. You experience all the things about yourself that you don't get the chance to when the straight people are doing it. When they're fourteen, fifteen, sixteen, they're learning about dating, and they're learning about the opposite sex and relationships. Even if you have a girlfriend in high school, it is so much different. I had a girlfriend in junior high and most of high school, and it wasn't the same. With her I had a very strong relationship, but as soon as sex came into the picture, I couldn't do it. Up to the point I was 21, I never had anyone to talk to about my feelings and what was going on inside me. When I was finally able to, there was a lot of the giddiness and the newness of the whole thing. It was a really exciting time.

The thing that upsets me the most is when people ask me, "When did you choose that lifestyle?" because I didn't have the choice. Why would someone choose a lifestyle of persecution--a lifestyle that means that you will never be allowed to marry the person you want to be with, that you'll never be allowed to have children, and pretty much never be allowed to be yourself in public? This is not a choice of mine. This is the way I was born. It's the way things happened, and I'm learning to deal with it, accept it, and to look at myself as being a special person.

My sister has three boys, and she has been very open with them. She told them, "I will love you, no matter if you fall in love with a woman or a man." She's been very supportive, and I think that's what's going to be needed, especially for young kids growing up. For me, the hardest thing was that I had no one to talk to about it, and I had no role models. I had no fellow students in high school that I even dared to talk to. I think if parents and other people can be more open about it and more supportive, it would be a lot easier for kids growing up, and there might be less teenage suicides.

Tim: I have people I work with that criticize my brother, and they don't even know him. They've met him a couple of times, and they're nice to him when he comes down, but instead of accepting him and being friends with him, they want to try to convert him back. I say, "Why try to change him to being heterosexual and making him miserable, when it's obvious that he's happy. He's not pouting around. When he does have problems with his boyfriends, he hurts just like I do with my divorce."

274

Jim: The relationships are the same, whether they're heterosexual or homosexual. The differences are societal pressures. I think that my first relationship might have been more successful, if there weren't those pressures. I was open with my family, but he wasn't, until after we broke up. I spent a lot of holidays at his parents' house. He's one of four brothers, and they'd have their wives there. The wives could show affection to their husbands. I couldn't. I was always introduced as the roommate. Come on, folks, wake up. I've been living with this person for seven years in four different cities. So I was resentful. I felt cheated. I wanted some respect. Those kind of things put stress on a relationship.

Tim: People don't accept gays and lesbians, because they think they can catch it by making contact with them, like it's some kind of disease or something: "I don't want to deal with him; I don't want to catch being gay." That's one of the stereotypes of a guy I work with.

The thing that bothers me the most, though, is the ignorant people doing the gay-bashing. I'm a worry-wart, and I worry about my brother a little.

A lot of people know that my brother's gay and want to know how I can handle it. I say, "What if it was your brother? Would you get rid of him because he's gay?" You're raised with somebody as a brother and, being the oldest by 20 minutes, you look out for him. I've accepted it. I can live with it. The people who can't, that's their problem. It's not ours.

I think down the road, we're going to see more people accepting gays and lesbians into the community. I think the younger we start the children out, like my sister's kids, then the more we're going to see a difference; but we're always going to

275

have people that teach their kids the negative. The only one they're hurting is their kids. There are people who will understand and accept, and then there are people who won't understand and don't want to understand. It's like a saying that I read off a teabag my mom got, "Some people's minds is like concrete--all mixed up and permanently set."

Janice

When I was nine, I looked in the mirror, and I said, right out loud, "There's something different." I knew. I didn't have a name for it, but I knew. Then I got over myself, because when you're nine you have friends and you don't think about being different. You just do what everybody else is doing. Other things were important--friends and playing marbles and softball and building tree houses--but I have never been interested in men. It just wasn't in my agenda. Of course, you have a lot of pressure from your family to date and a lot of peer pressure, too, so you do those things because you don't know that there's anything else you can do. In the late fifties or early sixties, homosexuals weren't well known. Everybody was pretty much closeted. You had to find your own way.

The Sunday paper used to have an insert with pictures of famous celebrities: women and men. In my bedroom, I had the whole wall covered with women actresses. I think Kim Novack was my favorite at the time. Nobody ever said anything about it. They probably just decided it was a phase I was going through, but like all people, when you reach adolescence, your hormones start rushing and you see people dating. I was always looking and thinking, "Isn't there somebody for me?"

****

The biggest mistake of my life was joining the Marine Corps. Picture this: South Carolina, 1965, white provincial New England girl goes to Paris Island to join the Marine Corps. I'd probably seen three black people in my whole life, had never met any Puerto Ricans, never knew any *really* poor people, although we weren't rich by any means.

They ask you on the application form if you're a homosexual. For some reason, I didn't think it made any difference whether I was or not. I had no idea that they'd be doing witch hunts, so I checked off that I wasn't.

Boot camp wasn't bad. It was six weeks of having some person screaming at you all the time and trying to keep you in line. I got orders to go to Camp LeJeune, North Carolina. Camp LeJeune had 100,000 marine men on it getting ready to go to Vietnam. There were 100 women, and we all lived in one World War II vintage barracks.

Probably 90 of the 100 women there were dykes. I thought I'd died and gone to heaven. There were black ones, yellow ones, poor ones, people from Appalachia. It was incredible, but the barracks was constantly being broken into. Women were being attacked and stabbed. I was beaten up. The men on the base were animals. They had charged them up to go to Vietnam, and nothing was sacred. They couldn't seem to get a grip on it. The Marine Corps has a real funny attitude about women: "We don't issue a wife, so you deal with it."

I got real tired of being beaten up, so I said, "This is nuts. I'm leaving," and I went AWOL. I was gone for 30 days, and I got to thinking, "Maybe I ought to go back, face the music, and do whatever I have to do to get out of this situation, because I can't just keep running and hiding."

I went back and turned myself in. They don't put women in the brig, but they place them under 24-hour guard. I was confined to quarters, and I had to report to the person in charge in full uniform every seven hours.

Finally, I said, "I can't do this any more. I'm just going to go tell them I'm a lesbian and let them throw my butt out." So I did. They sent these two guys from the CIA over to see me, and they took me to the basement of this building, with one light, like you see in the old movies--one light and these two men. I had no lawyer, no representative, nothing. In order for me to get out of the Marine Corps, these two men wanted me to sit and write how I made love to a woman. They wanted me to name the women that I was living with in the barracks. This went on day after day after day. They went through all my belongings. I had gathered a big notebook full of old folk and country songs that were popular. They took that, and they never gave it back. They took all my letters. They took everything. It took me three or four months to get out. It was the worst thing that I have ever had to face.

****

Recently, I kind of wished I'd had children, which is interesting, because I didn't think that I would go through that. It was brief, and I didn't perseverate on it for very long.

When I was 32, I was with a woman who was 40, and she wanted to have children. She decided that because we were so different emotionally--I was more of a caregiver, and she was more of a thinker and a doer--that we'd be good for a child. So in 1977, we decided that she would be artificially inseminated. She went down to New York City to the sperm bank and was interviewed. They okayed it and shipped the sperm from New York on the bus. I inseminated her, and she had a beautiful baby girl.

Then I was going to get pregnant, so that we'd have two children. But about six months after the baby was born, she decided that I wasn't what she really wanted, so she threw me out. It's bad enough losing one person, but when you've got to lose a person and a baby, it was a tough time. I thought about adoption, but that too passed, so I'm recovered. I'm a recovered mother.

If I'd had a choice, I would not have chosen to be a lesbian, because life has not been easy, but I didn't have a choice. You might have a choice about whether you get married, have children, and suppress those feelings, but when I was born, I was born a lesbian. You have to deal with what you've got. I get real tired of people saying, "You could change your ways."

In all the places that I've worked, you can't say 'we,' because people then want to know. You can't share the joys or the sorrows; you can't be mad if you're having a fight. There's nobody you can go to and say, "She's being a jerk." Even though they're wonderful, that's something that just doesn't happen. They talk about their husbands and what's happening in their relationships, but it's almost like, "I can accept that you're a lesbian, but I don't want to hear about your pain or that you have a life."

I think everybody's looking for a relationship that will last. As you get older, I think that desire gets worse. I'd like to spend the next 30 or 40 years--however much time I've got left--with somebody. I think my worst fear is that some day I'm going to be old and be put into a nursing home full of homophobic straight women and not be able to share my stories or be who I am. That's a big fear.

Tom and Phil

Phil: We met through friends. We knew each other six months before we knew we wanted to be together for life. I fell in love with him first--that first moment, that first Friday night.

I had all this free time, so I'd call him every night. I was living in an apartment, so I had no lawn to cut, and I didn't have yard work. You own a home, and you always have something to do.

Tom: I was a very independent person at the time, and Phil kept coming out. It was so hard, because sometimes I'd work late, and I'd just get home and try to pick up things, change, take a shower, and he'd call and be over. I wanted to be with him, but I also wanted to get stuff done. He, of course, wasn't used to being out here, so he needed my attention the whole time.

Phil: I was content just to be here. When you're in love, you're just content to be near the person. That's what love is--not the sexual. I knew it wasn't infatuation, because you *know* when you fall in love with someone. I think everybody knows. I certainly knew.

Tom: It wasn't until he put on a surprise birthday party for me and all these people came over. I saw him sitting on the porch all by himself, and he was content. I was out there with everybody else, and I thought, "Wow, he's happy; he's satisfied; he can do something on his own here." For the first time, I thought, "I'm in love with him." It took almost six months, and then it just hit me right there.

I think we get along so well, because we are opposite in a lot of things we like to do. He likes to do housework; I'd rather do the yard work. We also love to go on trips together. It works out super.

Phil: I can't imagine what my life would be like without him. We go hiking and mountain climbing together every summer. It's always like our first time together. It's like being little kids, but at the same time, we enjoy best what we do at home.

Tom: We're pretty much home people. We always eat in. He's a super cook. He cooks tremendous Vietnamese meals, and I cook the boring American ones to fill in here and there. We don't enjoy going out, because of the way society treats us. We love to go out with another couple and have a meal once every couple months, but it feels better if four of us go out. He feels more uncomfortable than I do, but we both would rather get together with our friends, probably once a month at somebody's house, and have a grand time cooking a big feast.

Phil: We always get together here at night, sit down, watch TV for an hour, and then just talk. We always go to bed at the same time. We don't go in there to have sex. We just lie there and put our arms around each other and talk maybe ten or fifteen minutes and then kiss good night, turn over, and flick off the light.

****

Phil: Growing up was like a jigsaw puzzle with all four corners missing. Growing up gay and trying to put it together just doesn't fit. You have to be satisfied with a puzzle with the four corners missing. It's not going to be the whole.

I was raised in Saigon, Vietnam. My mother was half French and half Vietnamese. I was aware that I was gay from the time I was four or five, but it wasn't that big of a deal then. I felt the sexual attraction that young, even though physically I wasn't able to. Emotionally, though, I was geared toward my own preference.

In Saigon, guys walking down the street would be holding hands with their best friends. Americans over there were freaking out. My father was American, and he freaked out, calling them fags and stuff like that.

I came over here when I was nine. I remember, it was so confusing. My father was a vet and was weirding out with post-traumatic stress syndrome, so my aunt and uncle took care of me and my brother. They already had three sons and a daughter of their own.

Their family is very macho oriented. Everybody in the family was a jock. I was involved with basketball, soccer, football, and track. Growing up there, I was perceived as straight. We won basketball championships and soccer championships together. I was a starter, so I was really physically athletic. I'm glad I was raised in a family like that, because now I'm not so visible out there.

I think the first time that I really found out I was gay, I was in ninth grade. I shoplifted a gay book, *The Joy of Gay Sex*. It's a real thick book, and it depicted sexual positions and explained all these terms. I don't know how the heck I got out of the store with it. That is the only thing I've ever shoplifted, and it was my first of anything to do with gay. My father found it under my bed, and oh, my God, I was so ashamed. When he found that book, my life just crashed. You don't know what that felt like. It was a horrible, degrading experience. I was afraid to death he was going to tell my aunt, uncle, and cousins. I thought, "now everyone will know I'm gay. I'm going to be the talk of the school. Everyone's going to hate me." The negative is all you can expect, once something like that gets out. Oh, that was so horrible.

Tom: I grew up in a very small town, so I never knew anything about gay people at all. I never saw them. Yet, my feelings go back as far as I remember, very pre-adolescent. My father's sporting magazines used to have a little Charles Atlas ad in the back with the muscle men. I used to cut them out.

I tried to date girls every once in a while in college, but I knew. I never dared to go to the gay meetings on campus, even though I had the urge, but I was in a fraternity, and it just never happened. I knew there were gay people out there, but they were very flamboyant people, and that was a turn-off. I thought there was nobody like me, who was just masculine. I was bummed out. I never came out until 1984, when I was 28 and out of college.

Phil: All we saw growing up was just the real flamboyant, the real feminine. That's all that was visible on TV. They'd show a gay pride parade, and you'd have guys with wigs on. That's what gay meant, even to a gay person like me. I thought, "That's not me; I'm not like that. I hate that." After a while, you turn that hate towards yourself. Young gay people like me, growing up, sit there going, "Good God, is that what I am?" Your mind goes loop-de-loop. The image you get on TV, radio, and the paper is that everything about gay is negative.

There's still all this bigotry and hate. Even your family, the people that love you, they're saying gay jokes, how they hate gay, and how they beat up these gay people. How can normal people hate? We call them "normal," but they're hating us because of who we love; and that's normal? That's not normal.

My best friend is straight. He's this very good looking guy. He's dated Miss Maine. We used to sleep in the same bed, but I had no physical attraction to him. There was no sexual thing between us. We had puberty together. We drank our first beer together, smoked our first cigarette together, smoked our first joint together, dated girls together, kissed the first girl. He's like a brother to me, but I don't know what would happen if I told him I was gay now.

If you're a gay person, there's a period in your life where you must deal with being gay, and you put your whole straight life on the back burner. My best friend and I lived together when me and Tom met, but I had to stop being friendly with him. I couldn't tell him. You either tell them you're gay, or you can cut them out of your life. That's all we have for choices.

Back then, it was easier to cut someone out of your life than to bring them in and explain everything to them. It's just hard to tell someone you love and look up to. What's worse in this life than being gay? Nothing. Nothing's worse than being gay. There might be a chance that he'll be accepting. There's also that one percent chance that he will say, "Get the hell away from me. I hate fags." With someone you love very much, you don't want to take the chance of being thought the worst life form on this earth because of who you love.

One thing that's weird to me is, how come when you see a man and woman together, you don't always think that they're going off somewhere to have sex? You see two gay men together, driving in a car or walking in a park, and you think, "Oh, they're going somewhere to have sex." You see a man and woman in a park holding hands, "Oh, isn't that romantic." Why can't we be perceived that way?

We've been together for four years, and sexually, it's probably only an hour a week. I mean, you're talking one out of 170th of our life and relationship is sexual. Just because we're gay, they think we're having sex all the time. We're not. What's important in our life is just like everybody else. Our family comes first. Our jobs are important to us. Our pet's important to us. Our lawn's got to look nice; we vacuum the floor just like everyone else. We have friends just like everybody else. We've got a life. Just because we're gay, it doesn't mean it's just sex. It's not like that.

I wouldn't change my life right now for nothing. I wouldn't change my past. If somebody told me I could change my being gay, I'd tell them to go to hell. I'm in love with this man, and I don't want a woman. I've accepted who I am, and I guess I'm finally realizing I'm proud of who I am.

Sarah and Debby

Sarah: This is a small town, but we were real lucky as far as getting support for our wedding. I grew up with my next door neighbor's daughter, so it was real traumatic for me to go and tell them that I was having this service, but I got over there, and they already knew. My sister came. Debby's sister and brother-in-law and her parents came.

Debby: I had asked my friend to give me away at the wedding, but I'm Daddy's girl. I knew my parents were coming, but I wasn't sure about asking my father. Then my sister called me on the phone and said, "Have you asked Dad to give you away?" I thought about it, and when my mother called me two days later, she was, "Have you asked your father to give you away?" I'm like, "No," and she said, "Well, I think he's really waiting for it." So I called and was chit-chatting with him, and I said, "Dad, I have a favor to ask. Will you...?" He said, "Yes, I will." I'm like, "Dad, you don't even know what I'm asking yet. Buy me a car." Then Mom called a week later and asked if I'd mind if she walked me down the aisle, too. So they both walked me down.

Sarah: Once that all happened, I decided I better ask my sister, or I was going to be in the doghouse forever. So I asked my sister, and it worked out fine.

Debby: One of the girls I work with, who is straight, sang at the wedding, and Sarah's bosses came.

Sarah: It was hard, though, to tell my boss so I could get the time off, because I wanted that week after the wedding off for our honeymoon. There was somebody else who had that week off, too, so we had to tell them why we wanted it. I told one boss, and that boss had to go tell her boss, and then her boss had to go tell the head honcho. It got around the bank pretty quick, but I don't have any problems there. I'm not shunned from get-togethers or anything like that, so I've been lucky in that aspect.

When I first started at the bank, I got comments, but as they got to know me and as time went on, the comments stopped.

The neighborhood got educated last summer. We spend a lot of time out here on the porch. We decided a long time ago that this is our house, and if they want to look through the windows, it's their problem what they see. So, we don't hide a whole lot from them.

I've been lucky as far as the neighborhood, because they've known me all my life. We don't flaunt it, but we don't necessarily hide it, either. We've gotten more open since we've gotten married, because we figure everybody knows now, so who cares?

Debby: I couldn't waste my time being closeted. It takes too much energy.

Sarah: For me, this relationship is a different closeness. The only way I can describe it is that it's an adult love, more so than what I've felt in the past. It's a commitment that we've both made and both wholeheartedly believe in. We'll always try to work it out, no matter what. It's a commitment to each other, to having a family, and to passing on the ideas and the love that we have together.

****

Debby: I was closer to my dad growing up, only because my mom's boisterous like me. If I have something to say, I say it, and that's it. But my dad has a real soft side to him.

My childhood was very twisted, though. My grandfather started abusing me when I was four. My grandparents used to watch me while my parents worked. I'd get out of school early and have to go over there. The abuse started because I had patent leather shoes on and they had hardwood floors. I kept running in and out of the house, and he decided it was too much noise for him, so it started with a spanking, and then it progressed over the years. It was my mom's father. My father was a state child, so I don't have family on that side. Mom says now when she looks back on it, she should have realized, because we'd scream and not want to go over. His reminder not to tell anyone was to pinch my butt. He'd hurt everyone if I told. First it started with, "No one will believe you," and then it got to be, "Well, I'll hurt them," which I believed.

My sister was insistent I was gay because I was abused. "When you get over that abuse, then you'll no longer be gay." I had a hard time with that, because my first girlfriend was her best friend, and how could she accept her best friend, when she couldn't accept her sister?

Sarah: One of the disadvantages of the gay lifestyle is that people don't come out to the people they know. If nothing else this year, Debby and I have done our fair share of outing ourselves to people who wouldn't necessarily come in contact with the gay lifestyle. My aunt and uncle are in their 70s, and they came to the wedding. They love Debby right to death, but if it hadn't been for us, they probably wouldn't have come in close contact with it in their lives.

Keith

I did drag the other night, because the bar changed hands, and the new owner wanted me to come down dressed as Miss Queen City. I went down to pass out prizes and stuff. I did my hair totally different than what I usually do. My mother can't believe it. When she looks at the pictures of me, she goes, "My God, I haven't got four daughters and a son; I've got five daughters." I said, "Only at times." I love doing it; I just love to perform. I've always loved being center of attention.

I just went out and bought two more dresses--250 bucks for the both of them. One of them has purple sequins that I wore in one of the contests this year. Also, the woman at the shop had just gotten this black velvet dress. It goes really tight and has deep purple sleeves. It had only been wore once, and she gave me a deal on it. I couldn't resist. My sisters are like, "God, you've got good taste."

Me and my father never got along. First of all, I was a mistake, but my father always wanted a boy, and then he wanted nothing to do with me. I have four sisters, and he would rather take them hunting, fishing, and teach them all those things that a boy does with a father, but he never did that with me. He'd palm me off on my mother: "I can't be bothered with you." So I'd go shopping with my mother.

When I was fourteen, he used to take my next door neighbor's daughter fishing and hunting, instead of me. I'd have to ask, but he'd just go up and get her and take her. It wasn't a sexual thing or anything. He just preferred the girls over me. I never knew why. I became a Mommy's boy. I had no choice.

Me and my sister, we look a lot alike, but she's a blonde, and she's a little taller than I am. She's a year and from March to September older than I am. She was constantly in monkey suits, changing engines and everything else, while I was always shopping or doing dishes with my mother. My father always said, "she should have been the boy, and you should have been the girl." I was like, "Hey, you got what you got. Get over it."

After a while, my grandfather--my mother's father--taught me how to hunt and fish. I'd spend all my weekends with them. They both died in '83, and that really caused me a lot of grief. They were like my second parents. They were always there for me. My grandfather was like my father. When they died, it hurt me a lot.

****

I've been single for eight months now, and I'm looking for "Mr. Right." Everybody does. It's just like a woman looks for Mr. Right, and a man looks for Miss Right. I've met a few people, but I'm not quite sure yet. I can be friends with them, no problem, but I'm looking for a relationship and these are not the person I want. I've got my ideal man. I like them butch. I don't like them queenie. I'm queenie. I can be butch, but I'm more feminine than a regular man. I want somebody I could go home to at night and cook them supper--almost like a woman and man's relationship. I'd settle down in a heartbeat. I'd move back out in the country, and to hell with the bar scene.

If I found Mr. Right, and he asked me to give up drag, I probably would. I'd get rid of all my stuff, but until then, if they don't like me for who I am, then they're not worth dating, because we're just going to have constant conflicts, and that's not healthy.

I'm proud of who I am. I'm proud of being a man, and I want to stay that way. I do drag for the entertainment, for the fun, and I enjoy it. It's not like I do it every day. I do it when there's a function coming up down at the bar. Other than that, I'm a man. I'm Keith. I'm a human being.

Carol

I come from an extremely dysfunctional, alcoholic family, with a lot of sex abusing that is continuing in some parts of the family. It's a very large extended family, and I would say that probably a good 75% of us were sexually abused. There were seven kids in my family--all girls--and four of us were abused.

My mother's family was Catholic. My father's family was strict Baptist. The whole family went to church every Sunday, and we had to go to Sunday school. Yet they drank, and they were abusive. Even as a kid, I knew there was something wrong with this picture. We'd hear that God's a loving God and all this, but yet I saw the pain all around me and what was going on with me, and it's like, wait a minute, the two don't jibe.

It took me many years to figure all of that out and come to terms with who I am as a person and with my sexual orientation and that it is okay to be who I am. Then it took a lot of counseling to deal with the sex abuse issues and to finally become healthy.

I got married and had a child. If I was married, I couldn't be gay. Finally, it was, "Wait a minute, you're living a lie; this isn't who you are," and I finally came to terms with it. I shouldn't have married at all, because I really was a lesbian and he was dysfunctional, but I was pregnant. Then it was, "Well, I have to marry him now; I don't have a choice."

At least, I had reached a point in my life where I knew I wasn't going to be physically abused any more. One time we got into an argument, and he knocked me into the wood stove. I said,

"That's it. I want you out of here." I went upstairs and just started throwing his stuff out the window. He left.

I vacillated between, am I a lesbian or aren't I? Finally, when I was about 25, I began to come to terms with it. When I came out, though, I took a lot of shit for it. Part of my family threatened to have my daughter taken away from me, because I was suddenly an unfit mother. My cousins, my aunt, and my grandmother said, if I was going to be a lesbian, I wasn't fit to raise a child.

One day, a group of us were playing a softball game, and my aunt and a male cousin of mine, both high on drugs or drunk or both, showed up at the game. He held me while she beat the shit out of me and called me a fag and a queer and then threatened to burn us out, while my daughter stood there and watched the whole thing. My then-partner and I decided it was time to leave. We sold our house, bought this one, and moved up here.

I think my daughter always knew I was gay. Not that we ever talked about it. From the time that I was beaten and moved here, I went back into the closet. I was really afraid for her. I was still with my partner, but I wasn't real open about being a lesbian. We lived together very quietly. We were very careful what we did and how we acted around the kids or anybody else. That was extremely difficult. I even had a few dates with men just to make it look okay. I had decided that if my daughter had to pay the price for my choice, that wasn't okay. That wasn't fair to her. So I stayed in the closet until she was sixteen.

When I first told her I was gay, it was just her and I. Her and my soon-to-be son-in-law were living here at the time, and she was pregnant. Her and I had gone somewhere together, and we were talking. She was talking about getting married, so we talked about lives and choices. I finally shared with her that, "Now that you've made your choice for your life, it's time that you know what my choice is." We talked about my being a lesbian, and she said, "Well, Mom, I always knew," and I think she probably did. Then she talked to my son-in-law, and suddenly, everything changed.

I became green and had two heads. She went along with him. They moved out and moved in with his mother. I wasn't allowed to call. If I went over, the door was slammed in my face. My granddaughter was born with a terminal form of muscular dystrophy, and they tried to keep me away from her. All of a sudden, because I was a lesbian, I was a pervert. It was like, "You're not fit to be around children."

My granddaughter was in the hospital dying, and my son-in-law set up rules for times we could visit. I broke the rules and stayed later. Many times I was there till two, three o'clock in the morning, holding her and rocking her. My daughter knew I was there, but she didn't share that with him.

The baby stopped breathing one night, and they called my daughter and son-in-law. They showed up, and he found out that I'd been there, and he lost it. He was real angry. My daughter and him got in a hell of an argument over it, and I finally said to her, "Look, you need to make some choices. It's not okay to keep me away from my granddaughter. I raised you. I don't think I did so bad. I don't see you being a lesbian." She finally said to him, "Look, she's my mother; I love her; she will always be my mother, and whether you like it or not, she is going to spend time with our baby." So I did. My daughter held the baby while she died in her arms, and we were all there.

My son-in-law has lived here since. He's changed a lot, though; he's grown. It took a lot of work, a lot of education, a lot of, "Wait a minute, damn it, I'm no different than I was before you knew." He had to really re-evaluate a lot of his myths. It took time. It probably took a good year before he could start relating to me again. It took my daughter a good six months before she came to terms with having a relationship with him while still keeping one with me, and that it was okay to do both, whether he liked it or not. Now, all of a sudden, I'm okay to be around my grandchildren.

The kids had a real rocky relationship with a lot of fighting. If my daughter hadn't been pregnant again, I wouldn't have let her move back in, but I have this real commitment that I don't want another generation to go around. While they were here, I knew that my grandson was okay and that he was healthy. They moved away four months ago, and I know that no matter how hard I try or how much I want to, I can't always be there to make sure that he's okay. I've had to accept that. All I can do is hope for the best. I call and talk to him on the phone every week. He tells me what he's doing. He tells me if he's happy, and he tells me if things aren't okay, which is neat for a three-and-a-half-year-old.

I don't have anything to hide. I think it's real important to educate people that we aren't different. We are just like you. People who have known me over the years and who I've come out to have said, "But you can't be." It just throws them for a loop, and it's like, "You don't fit the image; you're just like I am." "No fooling, we are; we're mothers, daughters, sisters. We are just like you." But people still have the myth that if you've ever been married or you have children, then you can't be gay. I know seven or eight people who have had to re-evaluate all the myths that they ever thought about lesbians, because I didn't fit the stereotype.

Are gay relationships really so different from straight ones? I think in some ways the relationships are easier, because who understands a woman better than another woman and your needs and your wants? But I also think that closeness and understanding can sometimes be a two-edged sword. I think with males and females, there is some distance and lack of understanding, which allows a certain amount of freedom, and you don't have that in a gay relationship. Sometimes there's a tendency to become over-involved or to lose your sense of self. I think what all relationships need, whether it's heterosexual or gay, is that balance and the ability to grow and to allow the other person to grow.

Courtland

I remember a day in second grade when everyone had been dismissed to go to recess, and I went outside. Everybody in the class had run out to do things. The guys went to the right to play ball, and the girls went to the blacktop to play something else. They all knew each other. I realized that I had no close friends. There was no one in that class who was at all close to me. I always look at that moment as defining, as me feeling alone and sad in a way that somehow, I didn't fit in. I went out and watched other people do things, hung out and felt like an observer, rather than a participant or a part of anything. I knew then that I was different. I just didn't know what the difference was.

At sixteen or so, I found myself in a little dive of a gay bar, praying no one would check ID's. I was ordering some grown-up drink and hiding in the back of the bar. Eventually, someone paid some attention to me, and that was my first sexual experience. It was not wonderful. It was not even good. It was not terrible, but it was very strange and awkward. It was then that I came out to everybody, except Dad.

I was the first one in high school to say, "I'm gay." I came out to all my friends, and I came out to my mother. She was not happy. Of course, I was also very militant about it. "This is the way it is. Get over it," which is not really the best way to approach these things. My mother made me swear that I would not tell my father. She said, "You've got to keep quiet about this, because they don't treat parents of gay people very well." She was worried about this being a reflection on Mom and Dad and that they did something wrong, and so you're homosexual.

A couple years later, while I was living back home, I started dating somebody. Fairly innocently, platonically, we'd gone to the beach one day and had come back to my parents' house and taken showers. We were naked, snapping each other with towels, and in walks my father and sees me in close proximity to a naked man. There was no getting out of it. His head whipped away, not looking, and on he went. I heard the footsteps go to the bar. My pal freaked. He got dressed on the way out the door and was gone.

I fussed and fretted. I heard Dad not moving. He's sitting in a chair next to the bar. I remember laughing, thinking this is so stupid; there was coming a day when we were going to have to have this conversation, but at least there could have been something really going on. I ended up going upstairs and sitting down. He'd probably had two drinks by that time. I sat down next to him and said, "Hi, Pop." "Hello, Courtland, anything new?" I can hear it, in the West Virginia accent. I said, "Dad, we can talk about this, if you want to, but I'm not going to force it, if it's something you just want to leave alone. If you want to talk about it, I will." Dad said "Well, Courtland," (and whenever he called me Courtland, I knew I was in deep shit) "I don't consider that a natural lifestyle, but it runs in the family, and you're just going to have to be careful about what you do in this house." What he meant was he has two uncles who are gay. They're his mother's brothers. I saw a lot of things in that statement. "It runs in the family": it's genetic; "*but* I don't consider it natural." How could it be both genetic and not natural?

I got out of the house. When I returned the next day, my mother was seething. "What have you done? I begged you not to tell your father." I told her, "Look, this was really innocent. It wasn't what Dad thought, but I think it's time that we had that talk." She said, "You're not the one who has to live with him." He was drunk for three days. I moved out and have not lived there since. That was eleven years ago, and we didn't talk about it again for all those years.

I went back to school and avoided any lesbian and gay organizations. I got sober for the first time. I stopped drinking for my mother's birthday. I had to prove to myself that I could do it. I was going to school full time, working full time, and running myself ragged. My parents and I were in superficial contact. We saw each other for holidays. Then six weeks before I graduated from college, I tested positive for HIV. What a graduation ceremony that was. "You guys have a great future ahead of you," and I sat there with my parents taking pictures. It was one of the worst days of my life.

At some point during that summer, I decided that I wasn't going to die and that I had better figure out what I was going to do. I had no idea, but I had this acceptance from Brown in front of me, and it seemed like, well, here's something to do. Let's get a Ph.D. What the hell. I started at Brown in the fall, and that kept me really focused. I was still working full time in grad school. It was a pain. Working full time, going to grad school, and running back and forth to doctors.

I tested positive in April, started going to Brown in September. Dad was in a drunk driving accident in December and has been sober since. That's four years now.

Not long after that, I got into a relationship with a man, whom my father loved. We became an accepted couple by my parents, and he was included in family things that we did. We went to dinner with my parents and did things with them. I could be open about expressing affection to him in front of my parents and was able to talk about that. Finally, it was no longer Courtland; it was Chuck and Courtland together.

He was HIV-negative. We spent a year together, before he became terrified about my status and about becoming infected, even though by that time, I was working in the field and teaching safer sex. At the end of that year, he ended the relationship.

We had just lost a friend in December, and about three weeks later, he said, "Look, this is just not going to work; I can't bear to watch you die, and I'm terrified I'm going to be infected. We can't go on." It was devastating for me.

Prior to meeting him, I had not been sexually active with anyone for the two years since my diagnosis. Then suddenly, there was this man in my life, who I told my status to and who was accepting of that. It was sex, love, and intimacy; all the things that I had really wanted before. But that only lasted a relatively short period of time. We had three great months. Six months were all right, and then it was a little destructive. Part of it was him being really terrified of me dying and an irrational fear, in my eyes, of being infected. He was practically putting on gloves to touch me at that time, and that was tough.

It was pretty devastating, feeling like I had finally gotten what I wanted, and now because of HIV, it was being taken away. Of course, I wouldn't have had it if I hadn't had HIV, because before it I was never emotionally prepared for a relationship that intimate and that decent. There are parts of that relationship that still stick out as wonderful things, but I felt abandoned and angry.

A few months later, after I'd gotten through that, I told my parents that I had tested positive. They had not understood what had happened with Chuck and me. I'd been working on it in counseling. I said, "Look, I'm setting a date for telling my parents. I'm going to make them dinner that night. I've got it all booked. Get me to the point where I can do this." It took me four years to be able to do that. I felt good about it. I felt ready. I felt great. I needed to do it; I needed their support; I needed them to be involved; I wanted them involved. All the secrets had to be wiped out. We had talked about anger; we had talked about being gay; we had talked about everything. This was the last thing.

I got up that morning and collapsed in the shower, sobbing, thinking about telling them. I drove to work, crying. All day at work I spent not talking to people, pushing people away. I was terrified someone would talk me out of it.

I got out of work, I made them dinner, and I told them. My mother said, "Oh, terrific!" That was the most negative thing that was said. My father looked at the floor, looked at me, looked away, looked at me, and had trouble keeping his eyes on me. My mother was angry, but she said, "What did you think we were going to do, throw you out?" I said, "Well, no, but this is the biggest thing I've ever had to deal with in my life, and how you reacted to it was going to determine how good my life is and how I respond." My mother said, "Oh, come on, we've gotten this far, haven't we?" In a funny way, it was very disarming, because I had prepared for the worst scenarios with crying and tears. It was almost a let-down, but overall, they were okay.

We didn't talk about it for a long time after that. I felt badly about that. I wanted to talk about it; I needed to talk about it; I wanted to lean on them a little more, but I couldn't bring myself to talk about it more. Since then, they've really loosened up and talked about it more, and they've been able to follow my health all the way through. They're very good about it.

They're not real pleased that I'm as out about that status as I am. I've done a couple of things for public television, talking about living as a gay man living with AIDS. I told them that I was going to be on a program called "Out in the Nineties," and Mom said, "Are you going to be talking about that you're gay on television?" I said, "Yes, and that I'm living with AIDS." Mother said, "Oh, where do you draw the line?" Then I told her that I was going to the March on Washington. I had to promise that I wouldn't wear a dress on television and that I wouldn't get arrested in Washington. Of course, the woman has never seen me in a dress, nor have I ever worn one, but I can't wear a dress on television. Even my mother has these stereotypes inside, that somehow I was going to go away to a march on Washington and put on a skirt. If I don't do it at home, why would I do it in Washington?

Probably the most significant thing in the last couple of years is that I fell in love again, for the last time, with a man who has AIDS. He is a man who, when I met him, had just been told he had nine months to live, but who is still doing great. It had been about six months since my previous relationship had ended. I didn't want to do anything with anyone, didn't want to date, and then I met Joe. Joe and I ended up seeing each other casually, as friends.

It became obvious that it was going to turn into something romantic, and nothing sexual or even very romantic had happened, but it was pretty clear to both of us that we were two people who wanted someone in our lives, but he terrified me, because he was so much more advanced in his disease than I.

I, who've never been sick, and Joe had been in and out of the hospital with pneumocystis a couple times and had just been diagnosed with cytomeglia virus, which usually concentrates on the retina and can cause blindness. The retina actually detaches, and that started to happen for Joe. That's when he had a catheter put in and was having daily infusions of a drug called gancyclovir, which does not make for romance.

I started to see him, and I really did torture him, because I was attracted to him in a way that was nothing physical at all. I just adored him from the beginning, his courage and spirit, and this wonderful feeling I got from being around him. He's one of the most courageous people I have ever met and one of the men I admire most on this planet. But when it came down to it, I would always pull back. At one point, I had just stopped calling, stopped talking. Here you are, obviously falling for someone, but you're not going to follow through, because you're afraid you'll bury him and afraid of what that will do to you.

Joe went into the hospital with Legionnaire's disease. I went to visit him in the hospital, and I went to see him every day. At one point near the end of his stay, I was curled up in his bed with him, when the psych nurse came in to have a "chat". The three of us had this chat, with Joe and me curled up in Joe's hospital bed. Somehow, it was then that I knew that it was hopeless to hold out, that this was pretty special and, in a funny way, wonderful. That was a year ago.

Joe was diagnosed with CMV in February, and he and I have been together since just about May first, so almost a year. He's outlived all prognosis and shows no signs of dying any time soon. He has a catheter port and does daily infusions of drugs, but it's been a wonderful summer. He'd come have picnics in the park and talk in intimate ways that I've never talked with anyone, which is certainly the most important thing to me now. We went to Provincetown, celebrated his birthday, and had a wonderful Christmas with my parents.

Overall, the best decision I've ever made was to jump in that hospital bed and stay there. It's been the most significant relationship of my life. I've had talks with him about death and dying. We recently made his will and did some things about his memorial service. It was really tough, but I was amazed that we could do it. We talk and have no secrets and nothing hidden. It's a wonderful relationship. I'm very lucky. He tells me, "I can't believe that you stick with me," because he's on two infusions a day of a couple hours apiece. I tell him, "I can't believe you stick with me." He's an amazing man.

Talking about this stuff is a little painful, because it's not going to go on indefinitely. If things go along as they are, I don't know if we'll spend another Christmas together. I think next year is very doubtful for him. That hurts, because this is such a significant, wonderful thing and something I never thought possible, and that's really tough.

I considered myself homophobic until about four years ago. I was a gay person sleeping with men and in relationships with men, but if anyone had asked me if I was gay, I would have made a joke. I would not have lied, but I wouldn't have answered the question directly. Now I ride around with pink triangles on the back of my car, much to my mother's chagrin at how out and about I am.

I would be miserable and unhappy and drinking like a fish if I hadn't been given some choices and had to get smart and get life together and get some counseling. I never would have done that, if I hadn't tested positive. It's strange, but living with HIV, living with a chronic condition, maybe even a terminal condition, my life is better than it was. I know that my life would be different. I would not be happy. I would be living, but I would not be in love. I wouldn't have the confidence and self-esteem. I wouldn't have any of the things that I have now, if I hadn't tested positive six weeks before I graduated from college. There's no way.

There are people who are in recovery today, who wouldn't be unless they had tested positive. There are people who went to a support group and, for the first time in their lives got some level of therapy or counseling because they tested positive. In some ways, it's a blessing.

I had a recovering addict tell me that his testing positive was God kicking him in the ass and reminding him that we all have limited time and asking him what he was doing with it. He's been in recovery five years now and doing great. He really feels like he would still be out there using and selling and running around, if God hadn't kicked him in the ass. I like that analogy.

Even the death of a family member or of someone close can make you look at yourself and ask those fundamental questions: Are you happy? Is this the way you want your life to go? Do you have what you want? If the answer to any of those questions is no, then that event can not only be traumatic, but transforming.

Joe

I think I will never be ready to die. I'm the eternal procrastinator. I would like to do everything, but there's not enough time to do it all anyway. I've been active with a lot of AIDS service organizations and consumer groups. If there's not that, there's doctor's appointments to go to and treatments to do and shopping and weeds to pull. It's endless.

You think you're going to die the next day after you get your HIV diagnosis. Back when I learned that it was over, I thought, forget trying to have relationships with people. Boy, was I wrong. To just say no is to deny what's really part of being human.

I had gone back to college and was continuing toward a Bachelor's degree. When I learned of my HIV status, I had to stop, because I was in treatment for depression. It's very difficult. What it is, essentially, is learning to live each day more in that day, not entirely, but more in that day, which is something our society has never practiced or understands. It's hard to teach yourself to live more in the moment, when society is so much the other way around.

It's funny, though, because when I met Courtland, after the first date, he started following it up and made plans for another one, but he reneged on that, and then he withdrew. He later admitted that he was scared by what he perceived as the level of my illness. When he turned and ran away, it was maybe a month prior to when I was in the hospital. He came to the hospital to visit

311

me, and I said, "What are you doing here?" He said, "What do you mean?" I said, "Well, after that schizophrenic behavior the last time we..." He says, "You know, you're right." I said, "I don't need this; I've been through that too many times already." He just looked at me and said, "Oh, my God." But there was some degree of honesty in all of that on both our parts. Courtland has talked about what he finds most fulfilling about our relationship, and it's that there's a degree of consideration in the other person that we've never found in someone else--a giving--as much giving as taking.

You do have to learn to trust your instincts. It takes courage, because nobody wants to be left alone, and you're afraid that if you expose yourself as being that discerning, or if you're not willing to settle for crap, then you're going to be accepted by fewer people. In reality, though, the caliber of the people you're accepted by is more in line with what you were hoping for. You can really only be true to yourself. I don't think you're ever going to regret that.

****

When I was a freshman in high school, my father got very sick with cancer, and he died in the summer of that year. My mother was always a very dependent kind of person, and she didn't do well at all with his death and all the responsibilities. She had a breakdown that year, within a few months of when he died.

She had been an alcoholic for some time, so there was a whole thing with that, too. Growing up with that kind of thing, I really have a hard time isolating where feelings of shame and guilt came from, whether it was from knowing that I was different with my sexuality or whether it was from the shame of trying to hide alcoholism. I had a good relationship with my mother. I was close

312

to her and very dependent on her emotionally, so I really internalized all the alcoholism stuff.

In any case, within the year, she took her own life. The night before she took her life, we went out to the theater. I can see now that it was kind of a coincidental thing. It didn't have a lot of meaning to her, but to me, at the time, it was devastating that the next day, it was like desertion--complete and utter desertion.

As I went through high school, I had close friends, one of whom I felt very bonded with and very close to and would like to have had a sexual relationship with, but things then were very difficult to even think about or admit. One of my very close friends actually came out in high school, and the ramifications of that were so devastating that it really didn't make it possible for me to come out. He was ostracized and ridiculed and after that, didn't even hang around with anybody in school any more.

Then I started spending more time with this other guy. I just felt real close to him at that point in time, because he understood everything in my history, and how do you feel ashamed with someone who knows everything about you and accepts you anyway? So, at one point, shortly after high school graduation, we went out and got drunk. I made advances, and he responded to them. But after we had an intimacy, he had to deny it. He goes, "I've had these experiences, but this is not something that I can choose for my life." That put a real schism in our relationship. It was unfortunate, I think, that we couldn't really come to terms with that.

When I was in college, I made the conscious choice to make friends with people I knew were gay and to find out how to meet other gay people. It really wasn't that difficult. Making the decision to acknowledge homosexuality wasn't like giving up this wonderfully rosy picture of life in an affluent suburb with parents to disappoint.

One semester I moved into an apartment, and one of the people who lived in the next apartment appeared to be a gay person. He ended up being the person who brought me out. He and I spent maybe six months together, and then he was attracted to this other guy and took up with him, so I was left out in the cold. That was pretty devastating, because it was my first experience of being deserted by someone that I chose and who I felt cared for me. He was a very nice person and very giving. He wasn't cruel at all about any part of it.

Coming out was like a wonderful validation of me as a person. Being able to feel genuine affection or love for somebody and not be as ashamed of it as I may have been, even if it was only acknowledging it for myself and with that person, was enough to be really nurturing. It was part of a catharsis that was going on at that time, where I was beginning to understand myself in relation to society and starting to define what my niche would be.

My inclination was to have a deeper relationship with someone, sharing some intimacy. I wanted a traditional kind of relationship, only with a man. I really couldn't understand why some of the men I was involved with didn't want to explore a really committed relationship. Maybe it was because at that point, we were young, and that's not what a lot of young people think about, or maybe it was because some of the gay people knew that that wasn't easy, so they just went from these short-term casual relationships where they could experience some intimacy, on to others, never really having to commit to all the things which give you away. When you start spending a lot of time and you enter into a serious kind of relationship, regardless of what the sexes are, people begin to see you as a couple, and then it requires coming out in various ways and forms.

Very often, gay people can be in your lives and you not really know it for a long time. When I was working doing taxes, I didn't feel comfortable about being out at all. I think the human services field is different, though, in that even the people who aren't non-traditional have more acceptance of gay people, because they're around them all the time, and they realize that they're "just like us" in many ways; it's just that they happen to sleep with a woman or a man, instead of the other. Eventually, it comes down to the fact that you learn enough about a person to realize that they recognize the humanity in you, as much as you do in them.

(Joe died on July 8, 1994, one year after this interview took place.)

My world is known to but a few.
I exist solely on the sound of the surf's breath
And in pursuit of sand-castles.

If you've known the Sea
Its strength...its tranquility...its gift of life
You've seen my world
But have you felt it?

Come stand and stare
Allowing all sea noise and the sandwind
To engulf your being.
And if you let yourself,
Exist with yourself for but a fleeting moment...
You've found my world.

Welcome.

-- Gordon Barker

ABOUT THE INTERVIEWS

The stories in this book are those of 70 gay and lesbian people who volunteered to talk about their lives as they live and feel them. They are distilled from interviews conducted by Liz Sherblom between February and June of 1993 in the Northeastern United States. Although they have been edited for brevity and narrative focus, they are in the participants' own words. We have made every effort to maintain the spirit of each person and the context of their words.

Each chapter represents an individual interview and has been approved for inclusion in the book by the participant(s). Some names have been changed for the sake of privacy; others, following the participant's preference, have not.

We met these people through networks of friends and acquaintances who knew people interested in being interviewed. We knew one or two gay people in several different geographic locations in the northeastern United States and interviewed them. They, in turn, talked to people they knew, who talked to people they knew, and those who were interested called us requesting an interview. We interviewed all those who called, until we had reached the number we felt we could reasonably include in the book.

With one exception, all the participants were caucasian but ranged in age from their early twenties to nearly eighty years old. They came from a wide range of socio-economic backgrounds, from poverty to wealth and from relatively uneducated to highly educated. In addition to the 70 gay people interviewed, two "straight" twin brothers of two participants were interviewed with their brothers. People were interviewed individually or as couples, according to their choice. Most of the interviews lasted between two and four hours, and most were completed in one session.

Participants were asked to just talk about their lives from earliest memories to the present in whatever order and in whatever way felt most comfortable to them. The narrative was to be on the entirety of their lives, with sexual orientation included only as it affected that story. In most cases, however, because of the cultural environment in which we live and because that was the basis on which they were being interviewed, that was a prominent part of their stories.

Much More Than Sexuality is intended to allow people of all sexual orientations to get to know a number of "ordinary" gay people--people whose lives and values are no different from those of most others in our society today, people who could be and are our sons or daughters, brothers, sisters, aunts, uncles, parents, friends, partners, colleagues, or even ourselves. We hope to achieve a greater appreciation of the basic humanity we all share, so we can begin to dismantle the barrier of otherness based upon sexual orientation.

For Further Reading

For those interested in further reading on the subject of homosexuality or the ways in which personal identity is socially constructed, the following books may offer a beginning point. This is by no means an exhaustive list of the books currently available on these subjects.

Adair, N. & Adair, C. (1978). *Word is out: Stories of some of our lives.* New York: Dell Publishing Co., Inc.

> Based on the award-winning documentary film about the lives of 26 gay men and women. Interviews conducted by members of the Mariposa Film Group.

Bell, A.P. & Weinberg, M.S. (1978). *Homosexualities: A study of diversity among men and women.* New York: Simon and Schuster.

> (An Official Publication of The Institute for Sex Research founded by Alfred C. Kinsey.) Based on face-to-face interviews with 1500 persons.

Berger, P.L. & Luckmann, T. (1966). *The social construction of reality: A treatise in the sociology of knowledge.* New York: Doubleday.

> A well-researched, highly readable look at the ways in which our assumptions about "reality" are constructed by our participation in a particular culture.

Blumenfeld, W.J. & Raymond, D. (1993). *Looking at gay and lesbian life.* Boston: Beacon Press.

> A comprehensive look at "every major aspect of the lives of gay men and lesbians..."

Boswell, J. (1980). *Christianity, social tolerance, and homosexuality: Gay people in Western Europe from the beginning of the Christian era to the fourteenth century.* Chicago & London: The University of Chicago Press.

> "Historical treatise on the place of gay people in Western Europe from the beginning of the Christian era to the fourteenth century."

Greenberg, D.F. (1988). *The construction of homosexuality.* Chicago & London: The University of Chicago Press.

> An extensively researched and thorough cross-cultural presentation of the historical and cultural responses to homosexuality.

Gross, L. (1993). *Contested closets: The politics and ethics of outing.* Minneapolis & London: University of Minnesota Press.

> "...about the shifting boundaries between the public and private realms...It is a book about outing."

hooks, b. (1989). *Talking back: Thinking feminist, thinking black.* Boston: South End Press.

> An insightful, self-reflective look at growing up black and a woman in the midst of a white, male-oriented culture.

hooks, b. (1994). *Outlaw culture: Resisting representations.* New York: Routledge.

> A compilation of essays and lectures exploring the roadblocks to full participation by "outsiders" to the dominant culture in the United States, suggesting alternative ways of honoring oneself and one's place in society.

Kirk, M. & Madsen, H. (1989). *After the ball: How America will conquer its fear & hatred of gays in the 90's.* New York: Plume.

> "...trace[s] the deep psychological roots of anti-gay bigotry...outline[s] a boldly original plan for conquering bigotry by exploiting the mass media."

Lorde, A. (1984). *Sister outsider.* Freedom, CA: The Crossing Press.

> A collection of powerful essays looking at life as a black woman and a lesbian through the eyes of a poet and mother.

McNaught, B. (1988). *On being gay: Thoughts on family, faith and love.* New York: St. Martin's.

> A collection of very insightful articles written over a period of thirteen years for the gay and mainstream press.

Minow, M. (1987). Forward: Justice engendered. *Harvard Law Review*, 101, 10-95.

> A discussion of the search for justice within a society in which the very notions of right and wrong, deviant and "normal" are socially and politically constructed by those in positions of power and in which those constructions and assumptions have become invisible.

Miller, N. (1989). *In search of gay America: Women and men in a time of change.* New York: Harper & Row Publishers.

> Based on a journey "through small towns, farmlands, suburbs, and cities in search of the diversity of gay and lesbian life in America in the late 1980s."

Miller, N. (1992). *Out in the world: Gay and lesbian life from Buenos Aires to Bangkok.* New York: Random House.

>Based on travel throughout the world, looking at the social construction of homosexuality across cultures.

Monette, P. (1988). *Borrowed time: An AIDS memoir.* New York: Avon Books.

>A very moving autobiography of a deeply committed love relationship between two gay men.

Monette, P. (1992). *Becoming a man: Half a life story.* San Francisco: Harper.

>(Winner of the National Book Award.) A fast-paced, self-deprecating autobiography of a gay man, full of black humor. A very funny and insightful look at growing up gay in a straight society.

Penelope, J. & Wolfe, S.J., ed. (1989). *The original coming out stories.* Freedom, CA: The Crossing Press.

>A "collection of poems and personal narratives about the coming-out experience and its significance during four decades of lesbian lives and loving."

Peplau, L.A. (1981). What homosexuals want. *Psychology Today.* March, pp. 28-38.

>Discussion of research on love relationships of gay men and lesbians compared with heterosexuals and each other, showing no appreciable differences in satisfaction, commitment, and other relationship measures.

Preston, J., ed. (1992). *A member of the family: Gay men write about their families.* New York: Dutton.

>Individual narratives written by gay male writers about a member of their families.

Shilts, R. (1988). *And the band played on: Politics, people, and the AIDS epidemic.* New York: Penguin Books.

> "...a masterpiece of investigative reporting--a brilliant expose of the federal government putting budget ahead of the nation's welfare, health authorities placing political expediency before public health, and scientists more concerned with international prestige than with saving lives."

Shilts, R. (1993). *Conduct unbecoming: Gays and lesbians in the U.S. military.* New York: St. Martin's Press.

> Based on interviews with over 1100 gay service people over a five-year period.

Signorile, M. (1993). *Queer in America: Sex, the media, and the closets of power.* New York: Random House.

> A compelling look at the homophobia of powerful closeted gay people and the resultant perpetuation of that homophobia throughout the media, politics, and the entertainment industry, exacerbating the homophobia throughout our society.

Weinberg, G. (1972). *Society and the healthy homosexual.* Boston: Alyson.

> By the author who coined the term 'homophobia.' Examines the causes of homophobia and outlines healthy responses to it.

Weston, K. (1991). *Families we choose: Lesbians, gays, kinship.* New York: Columbia University.

> (Awarded a Ruth Benedict Prize in anthropology.) "...draws upon fieldwork and interviews to explore the ways gay men and lesbians are constructing their own notions of kinship by drawing on the symbolism of love, friendship, and biology."

Whitney, C. (1990). *Uncommon lives: Gay men and straight women.* New York: New American Library.

> Based on a survey and interviews with over 1,000 people in relationships between gay men and straight women. Talks of their love, their compromises, their struggles to keep their lives whole.

About the editors: John Sherblom is an Associate Professor of Communication and Journalism at the University of Maine. Liz Sherblom is an artist and after raising a family, she spent eight years doing market research. She conducted the interviews for this book.

ORDER FORM

(For Orders from Individuals Only)

PLEASE SEND:

_____ copies of *Much More Than Sexuality*
      at $13.00 each $ _____
      (10% of profits go toward social justice)
Sales tax (Maine sales only): 6% ($.78 each)   _____

Shipping: $2.50 *($4.00 priority mail)* for first book,
      (Canada $3.50 for first book),
      $1.00 for each additional book   _____

TOTAL (U.S. Dollars): $ _____

NAME _____

ADDRESS _____

_____

PHONE __ (_____) _____

Please send check payable to: Audenreed Press
P.O. Box 1305, #103
Brunswick, ME 04011
(207) 833-5016

DISTRIBUTED TO THE TRADE BY:
LPC Group
1436 West Randolph Street
Chicago, IL 60607
Tel: (800) 626-4330; FAX: (800) 334-3892